MW01230856

Dark Psychology 101

An Expert Guide to Discover the Secrets of Manipulation, Emotional Influence, Reading People, Hypnotism, and How to Analyze People Using Psychology Techniques for Controlling Human Behavior

John Clark

© Copyright 2019 - All rights reserved.

The content contained within this book may not be reproduced, duplicated or transmitted without direct written permission from the author or the publisher.

Under no circumstances will any blame or legal responsibility be held against the publisher, or author, for any damages, reparation, or monetary loss due to the information contained within this book. Either directly or indirectly.

Legal Notice:

This book is copyright protected. This book is only for personal use. You cannot amend, distribute, sell, use, quote or paraphrase any part, or the content within this book, without the consent of the author or publisher.

Disclaimer Notice:

Please note the information contained within this document is for educational and entertainment purposes only. All effort has been executed to present accurate, up to date, and reliable, complete information. No warranties of any kind are declared or implied. Readers acknowledge that the author is not engaging in the rendering of legal, financial, medical or professional advice. The content within this book has been derived from various sources. Please consult a licensed professional before attempting any techniques outlined in this book.

By reading this document, the reader agrees that under no circumstances is the author responsible for any losses, direct or indirect, which are incurred as a result of the use of information contained within this document, including, but not limited to, — errors, omissions, or inaccuracies.

Table of Contents

Introduction..2

Chapter 1: Essential Knowledge 4

Emotions..4

List of Emotions 5

Empathy 7

Manipulation vs. Persuasion 10

Ethics 12

Chapter 2: Analyzing and Understanding Body Language and Behaviors 14

Facial Expressions... 15

Body Posture...23

Gestures 29

Physical Contact..29

Voice... 30

Proximity 30

Deceitful Body Language 30

Chapter 3: Covert Manipulation....................................33

Defining Covert Manipulation 33

Steps for Covert Manipulation................35

Techniques for Covert Manipulation 40

Chapter 4: Dark Persuasion...44

Principles of Persuasion 44

Benefits of Persuasion................................... 51

Persuasion vs. Dark Persuasion 52

Chapter 5: Emotional Influence............................... 54

What is Emotional Influence? 54

Principles of Emotional Influence........................... 55

How to Use Emotional Influence 60

Reasons to Use Emotional Influence 61

Chapter 6: Using Mind Control 65

Defining Mind Control................................ 65

Using Mind Control 66

Techniques for Mind Control............................ 69

Chapter 7: Deception................................... 73

Defining Deception 73

Types of Deception and How to Use Them 74

Recognizing Deception 78

Chapter 8: Seduction with Dark Psychology 82

Defining Seduction 82

Choosing a Target.................................. 83

Techniques for Seducing............................ 84

Conclusion 91

Introduction

Humankind has always had a fascination with mind control. Countless experiments have been carried out by governments seeking ways to control the minds of others. People have written about the concept of hypnosis and manipulating other people into doing silly, out of character, acts, such as clucking like a chicken while strutting around a stage. Mind control has been used as a plot point in countless movies. Despite this obsession with mind control, it is something largely deemed to be a fictional ability; people assume it is an impossibility. However, that could not be further from the truth.

There are ways to essentially hijack the mind of someone else, inserting thoughts and feeling into their mind, tricking them into believing the thoughts and feelings are their own. There are ways to influence and persuade others into obeying mindlessly, and while these people may not be mind-controlled in the sense often seen in movies—walking around with a blank, glazed expression and not capable of anything they are not explicitly told to do—the mind is actually surprisingly easy to influence.

Dark psychology seeks to understand this art, to recognize just how far one can push their cognitive abilities. It involves understanding the intricacies of the human mind and understanding how to install the strings necessary to control another person's actions from hijacking their unconscious mind. Despite just how insidious this sounds, it happens every day, even in the most innocuous of settings. Even ads on television tap into this power of dark psychology, harnessing the understanding of the human mind in order to get desired results—and it works.

This book will teach you everything you need to know about the intricacies of dark psychology, ranging from understanding body language all the way to how to manipulate other people. Focusing on a wide range of techniques and skills, you will learn the steps involved in taking over the mind of another person, but also the importance of ethics when doing so. Some persuasion is relatively harmless, and benefits everyone involved. Other manipulation and mind control are entirely selfish, seeking to do nothing but benefit the manipulator. When you understand that fine line between ethical and unethical, as well as the steps involved, you will find yourself able to influence those around you.

Think of all of the possibilities if you were to tap into the art of dark psychology: You could boost your sales if you work in a commission-based job simply by understanding how to convince others to buy more. You could keep control of difficult or stressful situations. You could better negotiate contracts for work. You could land better interviews through persuasion and understanding body language—really, the possibilities are endless. As you begin on this journey, however, make sure you pay special attention to the difference between ethical persuasion and unethical manipulation. This book is intended as a guide that will be useful in your endeavors and does not endorse unethical manipulation or harm of others.

Chapter 1: Essential Knowledge

Before getting down to the nitty-gritty details, you need to first understand some background concepts that will be incredibly important to keep in mind during your conquest of the minds of others. Each of these is particularly important to understand, as you will require the use of each of these concepts to really master the art of persuading others. Emotions can be used to sway people one way or the other. Empathy can be appealed to in order to convince others to aid you. Understanding the difference between manipulation and persuasion can help keep you on the right track when trying to maintain balance between ethical or wrong.

Emotions

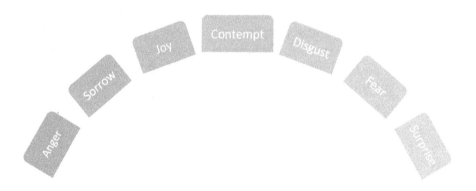

Nearly everyone has emotions. They are integral to humanity, and without them, life would be incredibly different. Some people are more in tune with their emotions—they understand what their feelings are conveying and they are able to regulate their behaviors that would be detrimental to act out upon, even though their emotional selves want to do so. Those who have that stringent control over themselves are said to have high emotional intelligence—they understand their emotions, how they impact others and are able to control themselves and sway the behaviors of other with their control. Of course, that control is not easy to develop—it takes time, effort, and mental strength.

Emotions are states of mind you enter naturally; they are instinctive, reflexive states of mind that are created in response to the world around you. These feelings come and go of their own accord, essentially acting as a translation service between the outside world and your brain. Your emotions take the sensory input from outside events and translate them for your brain, allowing your brain to create the appropriate reactions that will give you the best chance of survival.

Purpose of Emotions

The purpose of these emotions, then, is twofold. The first enables you to stay alive. Emotions are motivating—they are incredibly persuasive at convincing individuals to behave in certain ways. Think of it this way: If you are scared of something, your body is preparing to fight or flee. You take in more oxygen, your eyes allow more light in, and you are ready to move. Conversely, if you are feeling threatened, you are likely to behave aggressively to defend your boundaries. These emotions sway you to behave in whatever way is the most conducive to ensuring your survival in order to ensure that you pass on your genetic code.

Secondly, your emotions allow for wordless communication. This is typically in conjunction with empathy, which allows for the understanding of emotions. When you are able to convey your current needs to others around you, you are better able to successfully live in a group setting. Humans are naturally social animals. We live in groups, and because of that, we need to be able to understand each other at a glance in order to be more efficient.

List of Emotions

Humans have several emotions they feel throughout the course of their lives. When you develop an understanding of what the most common base emotions are, you will be able to better utilize them when attempting to influence or persuade

5

others. This is a list of the seven most basic emotions, as well as the facial expressions associated with them:

- **Anger:** The feeling of anger is typically felt in response to feeling wronged in some way. They could have had their boundaries crossed, or maybe they felt taken advantage of. Regardless of the cause, people feeling anger typically have their brows dropped low, shadowing over the eyes, with eyelids widened and their lips are held back tightly.
- **Contempt:** Contempt conveys a hatred or disapproval toward something. When someone is feeling contemptuous toward another person or thing, they usually have a neutral expression, with the exception of one side of the lips raising slightly for a brief moment.
- **Disgust:** Disgust is felt when something around you is going to make you sick in some way if you consume it. It is that gut reaction that keeps you from consuming something toxic. It usually involves downturned eyebrows, a wrinkled nose, and a lip raised upwards.
- **Fear:** Fear is felt when you are actively threatened or in danger. It involves eyebrows raised and eyes widened to allow for more light to enter. Breathing occurs through the mouth, allowing for higher concentrations of oxygen at any given time.
- **Happiness:** Happiness is felt when satisfied with what is occurring at that particular moment. People who are feeling happy often are smiling with a relaxed face, though right around the eyes, the muscles are tightened. This tightness creates the crinkles associated with happiness that cannot be faked.
- **Sorrow:** Sorrow involves a withdrawal in which there has been some sort of loss or pain inflicted. It cues to others that support is needed in order for healing to occur. People feeling sorrow typically have the innermost corners of their brows raised upward with downward sloping lips.

- **Surprise:** Surprise conveys a shock or startle—something that was unexpected has occurred, and has taken the attention of the individual, who is trying to understand it. Usually, someone who has been surprised has a wide mouth with dilated eyes and lifted brows and widened eyes.

Empathy

Like emotions, empathy is one of those things that most people know what it is as a concept but would struggle to define it if they were ever asked to do so. The vast majority of people have some degree of empathy, and for good reason: Like emotions, it has an incredibly important evolutionary purpose. It is that feeling you get when you look at someone else and you understand their emotional state so thoroughly and completely that you feel it yourself.

Defining Empathy
Empathy is the ability to understand, recognize, and feel someone else's current mental state, and it comes in three forms: Emotional, cognitive, and compassionate. Each of these types of empathy is incredibly important in terms of human survival, and also in understanding how to influence other people. This will be a key concept you will use to persuade others, so it is important to understand.

Emotional empathy encompasses the ability to feel another person's emotions. You hear what other people are saying and take on their own mood, sort of mirroring their mental states. For example, if you see someone sobbing on a bench, you, yourself, begin to feel sad as well.

Cognitive empathy involves understanding the thoughts and feelings of other people. You can see and comprehend what is happening to someone else emotionally and predict their thought processes, but you may not necessarily be swayed by their mental states.

Compassionate empathy is a sort of combination of the previous two kinds, with an extra tenet. Compassionate empathy entails understanding what someone is feeling and suffering through at the moment, feeling their feelings, and being motivated to help in some way based off of the understanding and feeling.

Emotional Empathy

- Feeling others' emotions

Cognitive Empathy

- Understanding others' emotions and thoughts

Compassionate Empathy

- Understanding and feeling another's emotions and feeling the need to alleviate their suffering

Purpose of Empathy

Empathy has a crucial purpose: Ensuring the survival of the species. It does this in three key ways that help ensure the survival of a social species:

- Developing connections and fostering bonds
- Providing regulatory feedback
- Encouraging selfless behavior

Each of these three key factors combines to create a species capable of ensuring the survival of everyone. By being able to recognize the emotional states of those around you and feeling the need to help people who are in negative moods, you are fostering deeper bonds. Think about it this way—you are likely to bond with someone that you stop and help, even if you had

8

no reason to do so. This is how you forge relationships; both parties aid each other in various ways.

By being able to see how other people are reacting to your own behaviors, you are able to regulate yourself. If you see that something you are saying is hurting another person, you are far more likely to stop if you can feel that other person's pain as well.

By feeling the pain and discomfort of other people, you are far more likely to aid the other people, even if it is to your detriment in some way. It may hurt your heart to see a child starving, so you give some of your own food, even if you may be struggling to feed yourself at the moment. You may have put yourself in a worse spot, but you feel it was worthwhile because you alleviated the suffering of someone else.

Together, these three purposes of empathy combine and enable humanity to live together in relative peace. When you feel empathy toward those around you, you are far more likely to help them survive, and you are far more likely to bond with them than if you did not. That motivation to aid others, that feeling of need that drives you to act selflessly, will help everyone survive. People are far more likely to return the favor when you are in a hard place if you have helped them first. This selflessness becomes a sort of contagious, and the result is a community that prioritizes making sure everyone is cared for.

Importance of Empathy
Empathy is quite important, particularly if you want to be able to influence others. Think of it this way: People are more likely to help others if others help them first. That alone is one of the easiest ways to influence someone into helping you. If you help them, they will feel an obligation to help you. Understanding how to read other people to ensure you are caring for them the way they need it is crucial if you want them to listen to what you have to say at a later point in time.

Typically, successful leaders are incredibly empathetic for this very reason—they understand the concept of I'll scratch your back if you scratch mine. The offer something up first, and in return, they get loyalty. They are interested in legitimately earning that loyalty from other people, and that loyalty they earn makes them incredibly effective.

Manipulation vs. Persuasion

Another important distinction to make before moving forward into learning the nuances of dark psychology is the difference between manipulation and persuasion. The two, though similar, have some key differences. One is used solely to benefit the manipulator while the other is used because an individual feels they know better than someone else about what they need or should think or feel. While the latter has its own negative implications that would send you spiraling down the discussion over whether persuading someone else to do something is paternalistic and therefore unethical, we will take a more straightforward approach. Manipulation is unethical, whereas persuasion can be ethical, depending on the context. There is a simple test you can do to determine whether something is manipulative or persuasive and it involves asking three questions.

1. What is the intent that is driving your need to persuade the other person?
2. How truthful are you being about the process?
3. How much does this benefit or impact the other person?

When persuading someone else, you are making it a point to look out for the other person's best interest. You are attempting to convince them to do or think something because you think it will serve them well. You are also more open about the fact that you are attempting to convince them to see your side.

When you are manipulating someone, however, you are persuading them to do something for your own benefit, and you are oftentimes quite secretive about your motives. You are attempting to fool someone into doing something that will either be to their detriment or will not benefit them in any way while benefiting yourself instead.

For example, imagine that you are a realtor. Someone comes in to talk to you about what they want and need in a home. They tell you that they have four children and that they want to be in a certain school district for their children. Now, imagine that you talk to the person and tell him that he may want them to be in a certain school district, but you have this steal of a house located outside of the district in a worse-performing school.

The house may only be a three-bedroom home, but you emphasize the space, the updated appliances, the land, and the location and really try to sell him on choosing this house instead. It is a good deal more expensive than the other houses in the area the man is looking at simply due to the land, and therefore, you would get a much larger commission out of it. This is an example of manipulation.

However, if the family comes up to you and the man says that he really likes this one luxury condo with two bedrooms, but is in the perfect location, even though it is going to be quite cramped, and even though it costs more than a lot of the other houses in the better school districts, you may try to convince him to go with the other house in the good school district that had five bedrooms. This is persuasion—you are attempting to convince him of something that does not benefit you at all for his own good. While you may be able to argue that this is infringing on someone else's right to free will, it is still arguably within the realm of ethics simply because it is looking out for the best interest of someone else with no regard to your own benefit. In this case, convincing the family to buy the house actually may have been detrimental to you—you likely lost out on a substantial commission simply by pushing them to buy something cheaper than you were confident would work better for them.

Ethics

Ethics, while important, are also quite subjective. They are the moral principles that define and govern the behaviors of an individual in some way, shape, or form. They are what tell people to behave in ways that are respectful to other humans. Unfortunately, ethics can vary widely from person to person and are not fixed. This goes back to the conflict you may have noticed between manipulation and persuasion—one benefitted only the individual trying to do the convincing while the other benefitted the person being convinced. Ultimately, ethics are a juggling act.

For the purpose of this book and to avoid a deep philosophical argument, you will look at three key points to remain ethical in what you are doing: your viewpoint, the other person's viewpoint, and some sort of solution that benefits both. Think of ethical persuasion and manipulation as a sort of compromise—in order to remain ethical, it must benefit the other person in some way, and it cannot only be done to benefit yourself. You must not use people as a means to an end, but rather as a person with which you hope to develop some further relationship. You want to help those around you rather than using them as tools to toss away when they have served their purpose.

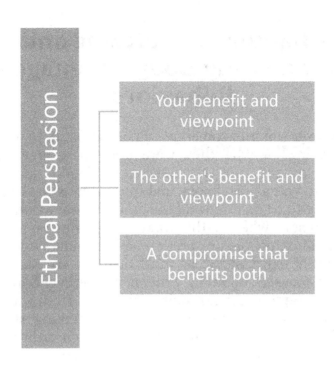

Chapter 2: Analyzing and Understanding Body Language and Behaviors

Have you ever run into someone and been unsure of what they were thinking? Maybe they were able to keep their face relatively straight, not revealing any details more than necessary to you as you spoke and interacted with them. Was it unnerving to be unsure what the other person was thinking? Or to be unsure whether the other person was being honest with you? Most people are pretty good at understanding and reading facial expressions, as most of those are natural and frequently focused upon in general communication, but if someone chose to withhold their expressions from you, would you want to understand what they are thinking still? The answer is likely yes—most people would much rather be able to understand what is going on in someone else's mind than to be left in the dark, and for good reason.

To understand something else is to be prepared. When you understand when someone is showing aggressive, assertive, submissive, or even deceitful body language, you are able to prepare yourself for what is to come, and you are able to cater to the feelings of the other person. Some of the language discussed may feel quite obvious to most people, but did you know that you can read a person by what they are doing with their feet? Most people never realize this, and yet the feet are one of the most honest parts of the body. As you read through this section, take special care to really learn what the various body language signs that are discussed mean. This is one of the most important skills you will need to master in order to truly persuade and influence those around you. When you are attempting to master understanding nonverbal language, you must learn to read six different factors: Facial expressions, body language, gestures, proximity, voice, and touch.

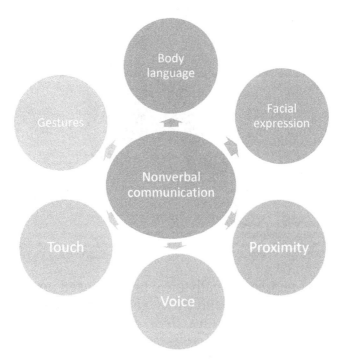

Facial Expressions

When you are trying to read another person, the most natural place to look is the face. The face can tell an awful lot about a person if the other person is not actively censoring it. The face is also perhaps one of the most expressive parts of the body— the eyes, mouth, brow, muscles, and chin can all work together in order to convey a message for you to decipher. Each part on its own may not symbolize much, such as looking at someone with a frown and not being able to tell if they are sad, angry, or afraid, but when you put all of the faces together, it paints a picture that can be quite telling. This section will give you a general idea of what to expect with the most common expressions, as well as some of the most common expressions of the eyes, brows, and mouth that can help you read other people.

Happiness

When happy, people typically have brows raised up, eyes wide with tight muscles around them, giving the appearance of crinkles around them, and a smile.

Sadness

When sad, people typically have their inner brows raised upward, and their mouths are typically downturned.

Surprise

When surprised, people have wide, dilated eyes, and a mouth slightly open.

Anger

When angry, people's brows lower, hooding their eyes, and their jaw may clench up. Their lips are drawn inward thinly, and their face may turn red.

Contempt

People feeling contemptuous tend to have a relatively neutral face with one side of the lip upturned just briefly.

Disgust

People feeling disgusted typically have a wrinkled nose, an upturned lip, and downturned brows. Their eyes may squint as well.

Fear

People who are afraid typically raise their brows and widen their eyes, which dilate to allow more light in. Their mouth may be left slightly agape as well.

Eyes

- **Pupil dilation:** Pupil dilation is a difficult sign to look for if you are not up-close and personal, the room is darker, or if the other person naturally has darker colored eyes. Pupils dilate in periods of interest, arousal, and fear. When pupils are dilated, they allow more light in, allowing for more to be seen. Because this is an entirely unconscious reflex, people cannot fake it. If you notice someone's eyes are dilated, they may be interested, thinking about something complex, or they may be attracted to whatever it is they are currently looking at. Conversely, narrowed pupils imply distrust or that the individual regards something as a threat.
- **Eye contact:** Pay attention to how much eye contact someone is giving you—it can be quite telling. If they are actively making eye contact comfortably, but in a natural fashion, as they are able to look away briefly and naturally, but continue eye contact afterward, they are likely quite comfortable. They are likely interested in whatever is happening, and this is a cue to keep

doing whatever you are doing. However, if they are struggling to maintain eye contact, they probably want the conversation to wrap up, whether due to disinterest, discomfort, or dishonesty. Hard, unwavering eye contact without blinking tends to convey aggression.

- **Gaze:** The direction someone looks is also incredibly important. If you pay attention, you will notice that people tend to glance at something they want, especially if they do not currently have it. For example, if you are talking to someone, and they keep glancing at someone else, it is likely because they would rather go speak to that other person. If they keep looking at a door or an exit, they may be ready to take their leave.
- **Frequency of blinks:** How often someone blinks, or how often they do not blink, can also be quite informative. When someone is blinking frequently, especially if they blink a lot for a short period of time and then suddenly stop, they are probably either stressed or being dishonest. People who are unblinking, on the other hand, are oftentimes being dominant, aggressive, or assertive.

Mouth
The mouth can be almost as telling as the eyes in terms of how much they can reveal. Look for the following signs when considering how to read someone's body language:

- **Parting tips:** When the lips are slightly parted, the person is likely attracted to the other person. They may be interested in what the other person is saying or be interested in a more intimate level. They may also be seeking the chance to speak if the person they are interacting with has been speaking for a while without giving them a chance to do so.
- **Puckered lips:** When someone puckers their lips, they are frequently either uncertain or feeling indecisive. They may do this while thinking about their

choices or whether or not to believe the other person. This may also happen in annoyance as well.

- **Tight lips:** Tight lips imply tenseness; the muscles in the face have tightened. This typically can indicate stress, whether fear or agitation or anger relatively reliably. Not many people can tighten their lips in a genuine fashion on-demand, so look for this one if you want to see if you have irritated someone.

- **Twitching lips:** When lips twitch one way or the other, it is typically nearly imperceptible and only lasting for a fraction of a second. It can have several causes or meanings, ranging from deception to lack of trust in the speaker, guilt, or even contempt and disdain depending on the context. Make sure you are looking for other signs as well when attempting to assign this movement.

- **Biting lips:** People tend to bite lips during periods of stress. They may be lying, or they may be anxious and uncomfortable with whatever is going on. Again, context is necessary to really understand if it is a matter of submissive anxiety or an attempt to lie.

- **Relaxed lips:** When the mouth is relaxed and loose, usually the person is equally as relaxed. The lips may also raise upwards in a relaxed smile.

- **Lips pulled back:** Lips pulled back typically mean one of two things depending on context—a wide smile, or a snarl meant to intimidate or scare away the other person.

- **Touching the mouth:** When someone is talking to you and touching their mouth, they are doing one of two things: Either soothing their own anxiety, much like how infants and children may soothe themselves with a pacifier or a thumb, or a sign of deceit. Their minds are unconsciously trying to stop themselves from telling lies, and it is shown in a quick touch to the mouth. Yet again, pay attention to context; oftentimes, the signs of lying and anxious behavior overlap a lot, even though the anxious person may be being entirely honest.

Brows

Brows also move around a lot during expressions. They can express an awful lot for something so small and limited in motions. Here are several of the most frequent movements brows make:

- **Raised brow:** When someone has raised a single brow, this can insinuate several things—amusement, cynicism, or even contempt if it is a quick flash of a raised brow that quickly defaults back to a neutral position.
- **Raised brows:** When both brows are raised, however, it typically is conveying fear, surprise, or happiness. You will have to analyze context to decide which the appropriate reading would be.
- **Inner tips raised:** When the inner tips are raised, typically, sadness is being conveyed. This is a movement that is incredibly difficult to fake or replicates and is usually considered to be a genuine expression of the emotion.
- **Middle of brows raised:** When the brows are raised in the middle, two things could be being conveyed, and they happen to be opposites: Relief or anxiety. You will have to look to other cues to decide which of the two it is.
- **Lowered brows:** Brows which have been lowered, especially when they shadow the eye itself, tend to convey dominance, anger, or aggression. This is even more accurate when the action is paired with hard, direct, unwavering eye contact and other aggressive body languages.
- **Furrowed brows:** When the brows are furrowed, the move together, making a crease between them. This is usually done to show sadness, confusion, or other forms of distress and anxiety.

Body Posture

Ultimately, the picture of the entire body is incredibly important when attempting to read a person's body language. You need to be able to understand what their hands, arm, head, and even their feet are saying in order to get a good idea of what is going on in the mind of the other person. This section will provide you with a generally open posture, a generally closed posture, mirroring, and an in-depth guide to the most common movements and positions of most of the major body parts.

Open Body Posture

Open body posture conveys openness and a willingness to continue listening. It is typically reserved for someone who comfortable, interested, and engaged in the conversation or interaction that is occurring and is a cue that the interaction is welcomed, and encouraged, to continue. The most common signs of this are someone who is sitting facing you directly. Their arms may be resting on the desk in front of them or on the arms of their chair, but are not crossed or in front of the body. Their feet may be facing you, and they generally seem quite relaxed in the interaction.

Closed Body Posture

Conversely, closed body posture implies a desire for the interaction to close or end for some reason. They are likely angled slightly away from the person, with their legs crossed or their arms folded in front of them. Their arms or legs act as barriers between the individual and the other person. This is set to convey discomfort, anxiety, or disinterest in the conversation and generally is a cue for you to either figure out how to get the other person engaged in the conversation or to end the conversation before it gets worse in some way.

Mirroring

People naturally mirror people to whom they feel a relationship or bond. Think of the interaction between a married couple—you may notice that when one takes a drink, the other does the same. When one person smiles, the other does as well. If one person crosses their legs, the others will follow. The reason for this mirroring behavior is because the people are close to each other. You can also see this with people that do not have quite a close bond, such as an interviewer mirroring the interviewee. If you are the one being interviewed and you notice that the other person is mirroring you, this is a good sign the interview is going well. People naturally mirror those with whom they are engaged or interested.

Arms

- **Crossed arms:** This conveys discomfort. The arms create a barrier in front of the chest, which is protecting the most vital organs that are located within the ribcage. This is usually done due to nervous or negative feelings, or when feeling defensive, insecure, or uncertain.
- **Crossed arms with fists:** If the arms are crossed and held with fists as well, the person is feeling hostile and defensive. This gives them the preparation necessary to swing a punch to protect themselves but also signifies the discomfort and defensiveness that came along with crossed arms.
- **Crossed arms while gripping arm:** This is defensive while also attempting to self-soothe. By gripping the arm, they are able to sort of reassure themselves that they are okay—it is them protecting their most sensitive parts while also hugging themselves in an attempt to soothe themselves. It is associated with fear, negativity, and insecurity.
- **Crossed with thumbs-up:** This is a sign that the person is feeling protective of themselves just in case something is going to go wrong, but they feel as though they are in control of the situation. They are confident,

yet still somewhat apprehensive about what is going to happen next.

- **One arm crossed:** When one arm crosses the chest, holding onto the other arm, the person is feeling insecure. Think back to childhood—when you were feeling scared or uncomfortable, your parents often hugged you to make you feel more secure. It is far more common in women than in men. As an adult, people tend to recreate this, sort of self-hugging themselves to encourage confidence and security.
- **Holding own hand in front of self:** This is essentially the male version of keeping one arm crossed. Men who are lacking self-confidence at the moment oftentimes cross their hands right in front of themselves, typically causing the hands to be held right in front of the pelvis.
- **Less noticeable arm crosses:** Particularly for those who are frequently in public situations, such as politicians or celebrities, sometimes looking unsure of oneself can be quite the disadvantage. A politician cannot come across as insecure, for example, or people will believe that the politician is incompetent. These people have developed several different ways to disguise the act of crossing their arms in front of their bodies, such as the following:
  - Adjusting a wedding ring, cufflinks, purse, jewelry, or watch
  - Scratching the wrist or arm on the other side
  - Looking at a phone
  - Setting a drink across the table closer to the opposite hand
  - Holding a drink with two hands in front of oneself
- **The Superman Pose:** This pose mimics Superman: Arms out, bent at the elbows, with fists propped against the waist, heads upright and spine straight. This is known as the Superman or the readiness pose. It is

meant to indicate preparation to act in one way or another and builds confidence and assertiveness.

- **The Package Pose:** This is similar to the Superman pose, but instead of fists on the waist, hands are positioned on the pants with the thumb looped either in the pockets or in the belt. This is done primarily by men and is seen as a dominant gesture—it is essentially telling other people to look at their crotch, framing it within their hands in a sort of dominance display. It is often done during flirting and frequently to make oneself appear more dominant and surer of him or herself.

Hands

Hands have an awful lot of language to share as well—due to the dexterity of hands, they are able to be held in a wide range of positions, ranging from fists to put together in certain patterns. Take the time to familiarize yourself with the following most common hand motions:

- **Hands rubbed together:** This is showing the expectation of a positive result. Think of the person rubbing his hands together in anticipation of the food the waiter is bringing out, waiting for him to remove the cloche from the platter, or the child who is excited to see what is inside a gift that is wrapped up.
- **Hands clenched together:** Typically, during periods of high emotions, hands get clenched together. The tighter the clench, the more extreme the emotion is likely to be. When you see someone with hands clenched together, you should look at the position of the hands to determine more— the higher the hands are clenched, the more negative the mood is. For example, hands clenched near the mouth indicates that something is being withheld and that something is typically displeasure and an attempt to hold back strong language.

- **Steepled hands:** Steepling involves putting the hands together, as if in prayer, but keeping the palms perpendicular—they should not be touching. The fingers should curve inward toward each other, resting on the opposite finger to create a steepling effect similar to the steeple of a building. This is seen as a position of power—it signals confidence and comfort in the position. When raised, it conveys confidence and can be seen as a know-it-all. When held lowered, it shows that you are listening.
- **Framing the face with hands:** This is typically done in flirting with others. It is typically done by women attempting to gain the attention of men. It is usually a good sign—it means the woman is interested.
- **Hands behind the back:** This is frequently seen as confident and dominant—it is exposing all of the vulnerable bits, such as the chest and stomach and is seen as fearless. It is done in three ways—Palm in palm, meaning the hands are together and conveying ultimate confidence and control, hand-gripping-wrist, in which the person is attempting to hold back from acting out of frustration, or hand-gripping-arm, in which the person is angrier. Generally, the higher the hand is gripping, the less in control the person feels and the more intense the emotions are.
- **Hands-on heart:** Typically, this is a person attempting to be seen as honest, as if he or she is speaking from the heart. However, it is easily mimicked and should be taken with a grain of salt.
- **Pointing:** Typically, pointing is seen as quite authoritative and dominant. People can make this become more aggressive by adding jabbing motions as well.
- **Temperature:** Hands are typically warmer when the person is feeling more relaxed and in control. When relaxed, blood flow is not restricted to the core, and the hands are going to feel warmer. When someone's hands

are colder, however, this is a sign that something is stressing them out.

Legs and Feet
Most people forget that legs and feet can convey a lot, and they often focus the control of their body language on the upper extremities and face. Because of this, the legs and feet are some of the most honest parts of the body.

- **Bouncing on feet:** People who bounce on their feet are doing so in anticipation of something. It can be seen as exciting, like a child who is literally jumping with joy, or as restlessness, nervousness, or discomfort.
- **Feet pointing away:** When feet point away from you, they are pointing toward whatever it is that the individual is interested in that particular moment. If they point to an exit, the person wants to leave, or if they are oriented toward another person, the person would much rather engage with them instead.
- **Feet pointing toward you:** When feet point toward you, however, it shows an interest in the conversation at hand. They want to keep listening to you, and you have the green light to continue as you have been.

Head
The head can also tell plenty about someone's thoughts, beyond facial expressions. Pay attention to these key movements and behaviors to understand what someone is thinking or feeling:

- **Nodding of head:** When someone nods at you, they are showing that they are listening. When slowly nodding, it shows that the person has listened to you and is patiently waiting for you to finish, or perhaps is mulling over whatever you have said. When the nodding is quick, it usually means the person wants you to stop speaking.
- **Tilted head:** This shows interest in whoever is speaking. However, in a group setting, people will

naturally tilt their head toward the leader of the group, even if the leader is not speaking. When it tilts back, away from someone, it conveys distrust, and conversely, tilting inward implies trust.

- **The orientation of the chin:** The direction the chin points is incredibly important. When it is pointing upward, revealing the neck, it shows that the person is arrogant or confident. When tucked in, the person conveys that they are uncertain and uncomfortable in the current situation.

Gestures

Hand gestures are another important part of nonverbal communication, but unlike most of the other types of nonverbal communication, gestures vary from location to location. Most people use them in some context, whether to emphasize excitement, disagreement, or other feelings, but they should also be taken in context. For example, the sign that means peace in the United States is offensive in Britain. For this reason, you should make sure that you study the general hand gestures that are local to you as well.

Physical Contact

How much or little someone else touches you can also convey a lot about their general thoughts and feelings. Think of the following contexts and what they convey:

- **Handshakes:** A weak handshake conveys a lack of confidence in oneself, whereas a strong one shows confidence and authority.
- **Touch to the arm or shoulder:** When this is done with just the fingertips, it implies that there is less familiarity than with the entire hand pressed against the arm, which conveys warmth and familiarity.
- **Hug:** Think of the difference between a one-armed hug meant to keep a distance and a big bear hug between

married spouses. The one-armed hug is far less warm and affectionate.

- **The grip of the arm:** This can be meant to intimidate or dominate another person, showing an ability to overpower.

Voice

Your tone is also an incredibly important part of nonverbal body language. While technically involving verbal communication, it is being included here because it is something that can be understood, even when the words themselves cannot be. Think of how timing, pace, and volume can impact how you come across. Someone can sound demeaning and standoffish through tone alone, even if the body language does not reflect those beliefs or feelings.

Proximity

How close or far away someone stands is also incredibly important to understand when attempting to read body language. As a general rule, the closer someone stands to someone else, the more comfortable he or she is with the other person. You can often see this with married couples, who may stand pressed up against each other comfortably, even out in public, without a second thought. However, people who do not know each other very well are more likely to stand with some distance between each other in an attempt to keep an emotional distance as well. If someone continuously shifts away from you when you subtly move toward him or her, chances are the other person is not comfortable with you and would prefer to keep a distance.

Deceitful Body Language

While being able to read people is incredibly important, it is equally important to lay out the signs of being deceived in one place for you. These are the most telltale signs someone is lying. Remember, a lot of these can have mixed meanings, so you need to take them in context, and remember that just because people tend to do these things when lying does not mean that people do not do these things for other reasons, such as feeling anxious or afraid.

- **Maintaining eye contact:** Oftentimes, liars know that people look for an inability to maintain eye contact, so they force the point. If someone is maintaining hard eye contact for abnormally long periods, they may be lying.
- **Blinking too much, and then abruptly stopping:** When people are creating a lie, they often blink more frequently during the telling of the lie, and then they immediately stop blinking and maintain hard eye contact.
- **Looking up and right:** When looking to the right and looking up, oftentimes, the brain is using parts that allow for creativity.
- **Body language that does not match the words:** If the person is talking about how happy he is, but his body language shows signs of discomfort, you have a pretty good idea that the person is lying. Likewise, body language may contradict other body languages as well— for example, someone might smile, but brows might not follow and the eyes may not get the typical creasing in the corners.
- **Stiff posture:** Liars tend to remain stiff as they are carrying the tension from hiding their lies.
- **Touching the face/eyes/mouth:** As briefly touched upon, people who are lying frequently touch their mouth, as if to cover it to prevent it from lying, and the eyes.
- **Fidgeting:** While some people may get completely stiff while lying, others will fidget as they attempt to release nervous energy created by the act of lying.

- **Arms crossed:** This shows that the person is feeling quite closed off and wanting to disengage completely, which people sometimes do when being dishonest and not wanting to give themselves away.

Chapter 3: Covert Manipulation

Covert manipulation is perhaps one of the more dangerous methods used in dark psychology. It involves systematically removing the power from one person in such a secretive, deniable fashion that the individual typically never realizes it has happened. They may suddenly realize that they do not know how they have gotten to a specific point in their life, and feel so lost and confused, but unsure what to do. This is typically considered rather unethical, but it is important to understand nevertheless.

Defining Covert Manipulation

When you attempt covert manipulation, you are attempting to learn what makes them tick so you can essentially dismantle them as a person and rebuild them into something completely different. It usually involves toying with insecurities so covertly, so secretly, that the other person never detects anything is happening. These acts are done in ways that allow for the manipulator to remain in control of the situation, but in a way that their relation to the event is deniable. This is done slowly at first, building up over time until the job is done.

In order to understand covert manipulation, you must understand what the words themselves mean. Covert refers to the secretive nature of the act—it is done entirely behind the scenes. The manipulator wants to remain the invisible puppeteer, pulling all of the strings while remaining as innocent as possible in the situation. This is done through hiding behind plausible deniability, meaning they can say that they did not do it and have it seemed reasonable and plausible that they did not. Secondly, you must understand what manipulation means—the act of swaying someone to do something that is not in their best interest and is not in line with their own free will.

Essentially, when you choose to covertly manipulate someone, you are hijacking their mind; you are secretly destroying everything they thought they knew and thought while doing so behind their back in a way that leaves you innocent. You are turning them into little more than a puppet with no free will, convincing them to go along with whatever you may be desiring. You are essentially brainwashing someone else into obeying your commands, into doing what you see as beneficial for yourself and no one else.

It is important to note that when you are attempting to covertly manipulate someone else into obedience, you are essentially using them. You are taking away their free will, their personality, and leaving behind a person that will obey. This is not something that you do to someone you love or value; it essentially dehumanizes someone.

Because of the dehumanizing nature of this, it is frequently employed by those who do not feel empathy—narcissists, con artists, and psychopaths all frequently use covert manipulation because they have no qualms about doing so. They do not see anything wrong with messing with someone's innermost thoughts, and will do so without a second thought, even if it is only to their benefit, and even if the only benefit they may get out of it is entertainment while the other person is left reeling and confused, unsure what has happened or how to proceed. It is all about dominating someone else's mind and seeking complete power against someone else. Once this has been employed, you are crossing a line you cannot uncross within your relationship—there is no longer love or respect; only exploitation and domination.

Steps for Covert Manipulation

While quite insidious, the concept of covert manipulation is also quite simple: It involves three steps. If you are attempting to manipulate someone, you need to follow these three steps to ensure that it will be effective and to your benefit. These three steps are the following:

Learn about the target
•Getting into target's inner circle

Gathering weapons
•Learn what makes the target tick

Breaking down the target for manipulation
•Begin utilizing manipulation tactics, using what you know about the target

Results
•Test to ensure target is behaving the way you want

With the steps followed, you will be left with a person who is so insecure and worried about his or her own ability to think and make decisions that he or she will gladly defer to you out of ease. It is easier to follow along with whatever you are requesting than it is to make decisions on his or her own, and the person will do so. What is left at the end is the puppet that the manipulator has been trying to create. At this point, the manipulator can work on fine-tuning the actions of the target, ensuring that bad behavior or not following through with what is requested is punished.

Infiltrating the target's circle
The first step to covert manipulation is learning. You must learn all about the target in order to begin developing a weapons arsenal that will allow you to ultimately take full control over the other person. Start by attempting to be welcomed into the person's inner circle. You must be able to be befriended by the target if you hope to be close enough to manipulate.

This can be done by pretending to be interested—in a way you are. You are interested in learning what you can use later rather than interested in learning what makes the person tick simply for the purpose of learning about the other person. When you are learning what they are interested in, and what makes them function as a person, you are feigning a bond between yourself and the other person. You want the other person to like, or maybe even love, you, while you remain in control of the situation at hand.

Once you are able to develop the trust necessary to be welcomed into the inner circle of your target, you will start getting all the details you want and need. This is when you will begin learning more about the other person, and the more personal the details, the more likely you can use the details as weapons in the future.

Gather your weapons
As your relationship with the person, or rather the other person's attachment and trust to you, has grown, you will start to get the crucial details. You will likely learn all about the other person's family life, as well as sensitivities, beliefs, and other deep, personal thoughts that could be useful later.

At this point, you are learning all about the individual's weaknesses. You want to know where all of the chips in his or her metaphorical armor are, and understand exactly what you will need to do to turn that chip into a crack, and what you will need to do to make that crack shatter the armor as a whole.

At this point, you are going to want to interact further with the target. You want to learn how to read his or her particular body language and tells as effortlessly as possible, as well as what makes the person tick and work. This is when you begin to understand the other person's fears, his or her thoughts, hopes, desires for the future, and anything else that may be offered to you. At this point, especially if you have been feigning interest in the relationship, or possibly even love bombing to push it forward, the other person will feel quite confident in the relationship. This is what you want—you want that comfort, that attachment, to build up, because that attachment is what will be your tether to keeping the person around, even through abuse and manipulation. When the other person is deeply attached, he or she will have a harder time separating out from the abuse, even if it is discovered. When attached, he or she is far more likely to stick it out in hopes of it stopping, meaning the tolerance threshold will be far higher.

Break down the target
The last step to covert manipulation involves breaking down the target. At this point, you know the person as intimately as you may need to. You know what makes their mind work, their fears, their strengths, and generally who they are as a person. At this point, you are ready to begin chipping away at

their self-esteem. Think of their self-esteem as their armor—the stronger it is, the less likely it is you will be able to install your strings to manipulate them. If you want an easy target for manipulation, you must destroy his or her self-esteem. At that point, he or she is not as likely to be able to resist the manipulation or stand up to any abusive behaviors. He or she will learn to trust your own judgment instead, losing the confidence in his or her behaviors that would have allowed for her to stand up to you in an effective manner.

Remember, this process is gradual. If you start out too big too quickly, the target will catch on and leave. Think of this as acclimating to water. If you are wanting to take a hot shower, you start with the water at a tolerable temperature and slowly work your way up to temperatures that would have been painful had you gone straight into them, and you would have jumped away from them. Your target will jump away from you if you attempt to go too big too quickly.

You could start out with subtle jokes—things that you can innocently deny. For example, if you are seeking to manipulate your girlfriend into losing weight, you could make a comment about pregnant women shortly after poking her stomach. She might feel a little insecure at the comment, and if she says something to you about it, you can shrug it off, say she must have been imagining the connection between the comment and the touch, and that she should not be so sensitive, or if she is that sensitive, maybe she should do something about it instead of sitting around and complaining.

This could then move on a step further—the next time your girlfriend goes for a dish that is unhealthy or wants a snack that is fatty or sugary, you could quirk a brow, almost in patronizing disgust and questioning her decisions without saying a word. She may then call you out on that as well, which again, you should deny, claiming you never looked at her like that. Remind her that you are not in control of her body or what she is consuming while speaking in a slightly disapproving voice. Considering she is likely to be insecure about herself at this point, you are able to slowly chip at her self-esteem without having to do anything extra. Even if you do not particularly care about her weight, this is one of the easiest ways to chip at someone—people are typically the most insecure about their own appearances, even if their appearances are perfectly fine in the first place.

Even further, the next time she orders something unhealthy at a restaurant, you could be slightly more overt, such as sighing in disapproval. When questioned, you continue to deny the action as being connected, instead blaming it on a long day at work or something else innocuous. You want her to feel insecure enough about herself to instantly jump to conclusions, and also insecure enough to not trust her gut reaction when you are doing something that is intentionally meant to make her feel that way.

The last step toward degrading her further and shattering her self-esteem would be through actually saying something. You could make a comment about how she always complains about her weight, but she never does anything to fix it, and that clearly, she does not care about the extra weight she carries if she never made an effort to work it off. This last step is likely to be far more damaging than the rest, but the entire point here is to slowly degrade her self-esteem down to nothing. Once it is at nothing, you can begin to put her back together again, installing all of the strings and buttons you need her to have in order to fully control and manipulate her yourself.

Because this has been happening gradually for so long and you have repeatedly denied any involvement with the negative comments or dirty looks, your girlfriend is not likely to associate you with the changes in personality that may be noticed. She may decide that she should be losing weight. She is also likely to be far more responsive when you do show subtle signs of displeasure. Even the slightest smirk or scowl, even if only for a split second, will be enough to instantly trigger that insecurity in your girlfriend, allowing for you to superimpose your own desires and beliefs in place of her gut reaction.

At the end of the day, the person can be trained and manipulated into whatever you may desire. Without a sense of self-esteem or the self-confidence to make her own decisions, she will naturally defer to yours, as you have established yourself as trustworthy in her own mind. She will take what you are doing or saying and go along with it. She will gladly go along with whatever you are desiring because she does not realize that the thoughts to do so are not her own.

Techniques for Covert Manipulation

When attempting to covertly manipulate someone, there are several different tactics you can use. Each of these different techniques can be different at different stages in the process, in different ways. It will be up to you to put together the right combination of actions and techniques to create a customized plan to manipulate your particular target. Remember, this is not a one-size-fits-all technique, and you will need to personalize it.

Love bombing

Love bombing will be particularly useful when you are first starting out in your attempts to get into the inner circle of your target. This involves showering the person with affection, gifts, compliments, and love in hopes of essentially addicting them to you. Remember, someone who feels a strong attachment to you is likely to put up with nearly any behaviors you may throw his or her way. What better way to do this than to essentially addict them? Love bombing seeks to utilize all of the benefits of natural love hormones. It essentially encourages the other person to pair-bond with you so you will be able to get away with virtually anything. When the person has come to associate you with all of the good feelings that come along with being put on a pedestal and admired, they are likely to want to seek out those good feelings in their absence. This also allows you to withdraw affection when necessary in order to trigger the individual to then strive to get back into your good graces by any means possible.

Gaslighting

When you are gaslighting the target, you are essentially making them think that they are crazy or unable to trust their own perceptions of reality. You should start off small—lying about where you found something, for example, or tweaking a small detail about an event you went to, such as saying that you got a bottle of white wine, not red, at that special dinner, even when you did actually, in fact, get a bottle of red wine. After refuting several smaller memories and creating the expectation that your target struggles to remember small details, you can start upping the ante a little bit—you could deny slightly larger things that happened, such as denying having said a certain thing that is completely irrelevant, or denying a thing that you did ages ago, even though you know that you did it. Eventually, over time, as you up the significance of what you lie about, you will create a person who doubts his or her very perception of reality. There will be no trust in his or her perceptions, which allows you to do something in front of your target and blatantly deny it has happened minutes later. This is particularly useful when you are attempting to break down the other person's self-esteem. Not only are you able to do so through making snide comments and poking fun, but you are able to eliminate self-confidence when you deny things happening because the person feels as though he or she cannot trust what is happening.

Sleep deprivation

Another common method of manipulation is sleep deprivation. It is used in torture for a reason—people become far more susceptible to persuasion when they are too tired to rationalize anything. Rather than being able to fight it off, they are more likely to accept what is being said simply because they are exhausted. Studies have shown that this particular exhaustion begins to take effect after even just 21 hours of sleep deprivation, meaning it does not take long to begin utilizing.

You could do this by making up reasons for the other person to stay awake. You could intentionally sabotage their sleep, or make the sleep situation too uncomfortable. No matter the method, the results are undeniable—your target will be easier to control when tired.

Threats of rejection
This tactic goes hand-in-hand with love bombing. When you are constantly threatening to reject someone, or withdrawing your affection to make him or her think you are going to leave, you are going to make them far more likely to go along with whatever it is you are asking them to do. Especially if you have love-bombed them and essentially addicted them to your love, you will be able to convince them to fall in line just by referencing the possibility of leaving them. They will want to keep you close, as you have proven to be a valuable source of affection and love, and in their desperation, they listen to you.

Criticism
Criticism is perhaps the easiest way to chip away at the target's self-esteem. Because people naturally fear and attempt to avoid criticism, when you actively criticize them, even if covertly, they are likely to feel on edge. Their self-esteem will slowly begin to crumble, leaving the malleable inner person remaining and vulnerable.

Inserting your own thoughts
It is entirely possible to install your own thoughts in someone else's mind through sheer repetition. If you can naturally slide something into a conversation several times, the other party is bound to eventually adopt that particular thought as well. This can be quite simple in a relationship if you are seeking to

manipulate the other part. Tell the other person how lucky he or she is that you are willing to be in a relationship with them. If you are constantly making small mentions of how lucky the other party is, the other party will eventually begin to believe it. This then sets you up for two things—you have raised the other person's tolerance for dealing with your abuse and manipulation because no matter what you do, the other person is still lucky that you are willing to be in a relationship, and also you are able to further threaten to leave. If the other person is convinced that they are lucky that you are there, if you threaten to remove yourself, the other person is going to bend over backwards to keep you because there is no guarantee of the next time he or she will get that lucky again, and there is always the possibility that there will never be a relationship to follow.

Isolation
Ultimately, people are the most vulnerable when they are alone. By systematically removing the target's support system through tactics such as ruining their relationships with other people or actively voicing your displeasure over friends or family members repeatedly, the other person may eventually choose to cut them off for you simply because they trust your judgment. When the other person is entirely alone, there is no one else there to point out any behaviors that do not seem healthy or right in a relationship. There will be no one else there to help aid the other person in escaping, and there will be no one else there to call you out.

Chapter 4: Dark Persuasion

Persuasion is everywhere around you. People use it daily and are exposed to it daily—they see ads on television designed to be as convincing as possible. They likely run into salespeople in stores and on the street that are hoping to sell them something new. Even politics and churches involve persuasion in maintaining control and gaining support. It is literally everywhere you look. Ultimately, persuasion may not be as insidious as manipulation, but it is still something that is important to understand, and it is something that you could likely gain great benefit from learning.

Think about this—if you are a salesperson, is being able to persuade someone a bad thing? If you are lobbying for a law change, is being persuasive bad? The answer is no—so long as you are doing things legitimately and ethically. In fact, understanding the art behind persuasion would actually be quite beneficial to you in those cases. You would be able to sell more, or get more people to sign your petition or vote your way if you are more persuasive.

Principles of Persuasion

Before delving into dark persuasion and how to use it, you must first begin to understand how persuasion works as a whole. Persuasion involves six key principles. These principles work together and make your chances at persuading someone else far more likely to be successful than if you do not implement any of them. These six principles are:

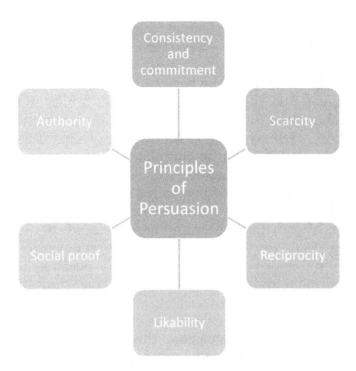

Consistency and commitment

People love consistency—it allows for predictability and allows for everything to be juggled in a way that is known to work. People prefer those who are consistent simply because those who are consistent are seen as reliable, which makes them trustworthy. Trustworthiness is an incredibly useful skill. Further, people like consistency and will prefer that over unpredictability. People want to be seen as consistent for that reason. This can be quite beneficial to understand if you recognize the opportunities for persuading others.

If you are wanting to persuade someone using consistency, you should first appeal to commitment. Commitments are important to people, just like consistency. Someone who breaks commitments is frequently seen as flaky or unreliable, and unreliable people simply are not as valuable as those who are reliable. The best way to use commitment to influence someone, then, is to convince them to commit to something. It does not matter what it is that they commit to—anything works here. For example, you could ask your office coworker to do you a favor and shred some documents when he says he is going to be heading to the back to shred documents. When he agrees, you may then begin adding other things on as well, such as asking him to also make a few copies for you when he is back there. He may agree to do that too, seeing it as only a few seconds extra for him to complete it and because he will already be back there anyway. You may then add one more step—asking him to brew fresh coffee as well since he will be in the back room. He may agree to that as well using the same logic—he is already back there and he has already agreed to do something else. Now, you have the coworker completing at least 15 minutes of your own work simply because he made one commitment and then wanted to stay consistent in saying yes.

When utilizing dark persuasion, through getting that first commitment, you are able to appeal to consistency, asking a little bit more of the person incrementally until you are at the result you initially wanted. Had you told your coworker that you wanted him to make coffee, shred documents, and also copy several documents; he likely would have laughed in your face and told you to do it yourself. Instead, you convinced him to do so by appealing to consistency and commitment.

Scarcity
People are quite fickle—they are often more interested in something as soon as they can no longer have it or they feel that their ability to get something would be limited. For example, when a restaurant or café removes something unpopular from the menu. Even by artificially creating a scarcity of an item, you can up the interest in something. For some reason, people will miss something once it is no longer an option, even if they never entertained it before when it was readily available.

Many restaurants take advantage of this by creating rotating menus. They will offer certain items as limited time only, advertise them returning for a week, and then run out quickly. This does two things—it gets people into the restaurant or store, and even if they run out of the limited-time item, people are not going to leave the restaurant empty-handed. They will instead buy something else since they had already invested the time getting there, which nets the restaurant even more money.

You can utilize the concept of scarcity in persuading others by appealing to limitations. Reaffirm that a deal you are trying to push is a limited time offer and really make it a point to emphasize what will be lost if an individual does not follow through with the deal at that particular moment. If you emphasize what will be lost, people are more likely to go for it. They do not want to lose and are more likely to be pressured into a mediocre deal out of knowing exactly what will happen instead of going with a fantastic deal that may happen later, with the risk of no-deal occurring at all.

Reciprocity
Reciprocity is a simple concept—if you do something for me, I will do something to help you in return. It is literally the concept of returning favors and can be seen in a wide range of situations. Think of when someone holds the first door through a store so you can get out—you are likely to hold open the second door for them to walk through simply because they held open the first one for you. The idea behind this is that favors should be done in return simply to benefit everyone. Remember the talk about empathy? You learned that selfless behaviors breed more selfless behaviors, which makes people more likely to survive in general.

Persuasion taps into this thought process—it literally seeks to tap into that impulse to return the favor. When you do something for someone, they are going to feel obligated to do something for you in return, even if it is an inconvenience for them, and even if it will likely set them back at something they are attempting to do. By creating that sense of obligation, you are able to get what you want, even if the other person would likely say no under normal circumstances.

Within dark persuasion, you utilize this to your advantage. Remember, persuasion is swaying someone to do something because it will benefit them. When you are using dark persuasion, you are also seeking to get something out of the exchange as well. You want to ensure that you get what you want, but you also attempt to do so relatively ethically—you do not want to be the only person benefitting, even if you are the primary beneficiary.

When attempting to utilize this, then, you should first seek to do something for someone else, and then ask for what it is you are wanting in return. For example, if you want your coworker to cover your shift on Saturday evening so you can go to a concert, you may offer to do a few things for your coworker during the shift—maybe you volunteer to take out all of the garbage for your coworker, knowing she hates to do it, and then you also volunteer to take bathroom duty. She happily allows you to do so. A little later, you ask her if she will work for you on Saturday, even though you know that she likes to have her Saturdays free for partying with friends. She is more likely to say yes simply because you helped her out earlier in the day by taking all of the literal dirty work.

Likability
Ultimately, people are far more likely to come to the aid of people they like than to the aid of those they do not. The more you like someone, the further out of your way you are usually willing to go to help them. This means that you are far more likely to be able to persuade other people if you are able to become likable to the other people. Luckily, becoming likable is relatively easy. There are three key factors that determine whether we like someone or not. If someone does these three things, they are far more likely to be liked: They must be

relatable, they must offer compliments or flattery, and they must be willing to cooperate.

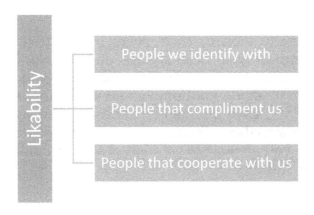

With an understanding of these three things, you can essentially convince other people to like you simply by understanding what makes someone likable. This skill can be useful far beyond just persuading others—you can use it to essentially convince them to allow you into their inner circles. When someone trusts you, and you have proven that you are working toward common goals, you are far more likely to persuade them to do whatever it is that you are going to need to be done.

Social proof
At its simplest, social proof is the concept of peer pressure. It is the concept that people will oftentimes give in to peer pressure when they are unsure how to act within a certain context. For example, if you just got hired at a new job and arrive at a room full of people with their shoes off and their socked feet propped up on their desks, all laughing and

chatting, leaving you feeling unsure what to do, you are far more likely to give in to what those around you are doing, especially if you do not receive any direction on what to do. Even though you may think that the behaviors are abnormal, you follow the crowd because they must know what they are doing.

People naturally look to their peers to learn—it is simply hardwired into us as a social species, and this can be used to the advantage of other people. For example, if you are trying to get people to sign a petition, you are far more likely to get signatures if you have the signature sheet on display, showing several other signatures. You are even more likely to get more signatures if you are able to get high-profile or familiar names written onto the sheet.

Ultimately, people tend to defer to their peers more than to their superiors, and because of this, you are able to tweak what other people are doing simply by setting up situations in which others are doing what you want.

Authority

While people are more likely to follow peer pressure when confused and unsure of what to do, ultimately, authority is perhaps the easiest way to get persuasive powers over someone else. People have a tendency to naturally defer to authority simply due to how our societies are structured. There is always someone with authority, whether it is a government, a parent, a boss, or a teacher, or even just someone who has more knowledge about a topic than you do. A doctor, for example, would be a great example of medical authority, or a lawyer would be legal authority. People tend to be far more willing to listen to the advice offered by an authority figure if they know that the other person is an authority figure, whether due to credentials being openly displayed or due to someone else introducing them with their credentials.

This can be incredibly useful in persuasion. If you are able to establish yourself as some sort of authority, even if you are not actually an authority on whatever it is you are asserting, simply by saying that you are an authority and offering even the weakest of proof will influence some people to obey you. For example, you may know a lot about computers but have no real degree—someone is likely to listen to you about computer advice if you offer up that you know how to put together and service computers, even if you do not know anything about the particular topic the person is asking about. The possibilities are endless, and for some people, even just saying that you studied something in school a few times would be enough of an appeal to authority for them to take your word on something.

Benefits of Persuasion

Being persuasive has several fantastic benefits. When you are able to persuade others, you are far more likely to be an effective leader and coworker, both of which are desirable traits. Those who are able to legitimately persuade others without the need for manipulation tactics or tricking someone into doing something are generally quite well-liked. They are often interested in the benefits of themselves and others, and together, they are able to create results that work for everyone.

This often leads to happier individuals who are getting at least a part of what they want in nearly any situation. Happier individuals are generally healthier individuals as well, creating even more benefits. This creates a person who is generally well-liked, happy, and healthy, which is quite successful.

Beyond that, there are four key benefits to studying and learning the art of persuasion. These are:

The instrumental function
The instrumental function is essentially the idea that when you learn about persuasion, you learn how to better utilize it. You are able to learn more effective ways to persuade simply because you know that you are doing it and learning about it, and you learn how to tailor your own persuasion tactics to the individual situation at hand.

The knowledge and awareness function
The knowledge and awareness function encompass the idea that the more you learn about persuasion, the more knowledge you accrue, and the more aware of the processes you become. You learn how to persuade as a reflex, something that is essentially as simple as breathing for you through the knowledge and the practice.

The defensive function
As you develop more knowledge of persuasion, you create the ability to defend yourself. When you are acutely aware of persuasion and what it entails, you are suddenly less vulnerable to the act simply because you understand what it is and what is happening at any given moment.

The debunking function
Lastly, with a mastery of the previous three functions, you are able to use your skills to see the truth in situations, especially when they feel like they are too good to be true. You can recognize the truth and will not be influenced by the lies that people may try to spin.

Persuasion vs. Dark Persuasion

With all of the previous information, then, you may be wondering what the difference between persuasion and dark persuasion is. While both involve persuasion at the core, those interested in dark persuasion do so for their own benefit.

Persuaders are far more likely to be doing so in a way that is morally and ethically sound—they may be persuading people to do something that will stop a war, for example, or enact a new policy that will benefit everyone.

Dark persuaders, however, do not allow morality to cloud their judgment. They see what they want and they go for it, utilizing the principles of persuasion. While they will gladly do the right thing when it benefits them, they do not concern themselves with making sure that the right thing lines up with what they want, and that is okay with them. They see no reason to force the point if it is not going to naturally happen, and so long as they are satisfied, that is all that matters. When using dark persuasion, then you are seeking to utilize the six principles of persuasion. Each of those can be utilized without qualms, with the decision that your desires are the most important goal to achieve for you. You may decide, for example, that you want to persuade your partner to give up their ticket for a concert the two of you were going to go to so you can take your friend instead. You know that your partner had been looking forward to going, and you know that convincing your partner not to go will be hurtful, but you want to proceed anyway.

You would then proceed to use the principles of persuasion in order to make this happen—you may go out of your way to do several things for your partner in an attempt to get reciprocity, and then ask for the ticket, or you may decide instead to point out how there is some other event that you are sure your partner would much rather do on that particular evening in an attempt to appeal to scarcity. No matter the principle you choose, you try to make it relevant to your partner in an effort to get the ticket anyway, which he may eventually resignedly give to you despite really wanting to go simply because you are asking him to do so. This is dark persuasion—you got what you want without worrying about what your partner felt in the process.

Chapter 5: Emotional Influence

Many people pride themselves on being rational creatures—after all, humans frequently justify their superiority through rationality, even if that rationality is negligible at best. They like to think that they make decisions based solely upon rationality. However, that cannot be further from the truth.

Do you remember when emotions were discussed and how they are major motivators for humans? Those same emotions can be tapped into in order to create the results desired by others. People can frequently be swayed to do certain things or act in certain ways through emotional influence.

What is Emotional Influence?

Emotional influence refers to the process by which people and corporations appeal to your emotions in order to sway you to do something. Perhaps most commonly seen in marketing practices, it works off of the idea that the part of the brain that regulates emotions is also related to decision-making. This makes sense—if emotions are meant to help someone make decisions that will make the individual more likely to survive, it makes sense that the same part of the brain is responsible for the processing of thoughts.

The way this works is with the theory that the brain works off of dual processing. This means that your brain has two systems that enable it to function—system one, which is unconscious, meaning it is automatic, nearly instant, and low effort, and system two, which is conscious, meaning it is controlled, but also takes more effort and is slower.

With the principle of dual processing in mind, you can see that emotions would be regulated by system one while system two would involve rationality and logical decision-making. Between the two, system one, your emotional regulatory area, is always running, which also implies that you are far more likely to make instant, emotional reactions simply because that process is already running in the background of your mind and it requires very little effort or time. Essentially, system one will kick in, make a gut reaction, and then system two will slowly rationalize that decision.

Think about two brands that have been largely seen as rival competitors, where people usually pick a favorite and run with it. It could be whether you are using Apple or Microsoft on your computer, or even whether you prefer cats over dogs. If you are asked which you prefer, you are likely going to reflexively answer one or the other without thinking about it. This is your emotional system one at work. System two, on the other hand, would then kick in and you would be able to offer the reasoning to that decision.

This idea that we think with our emotions first and rationality later can be particularly useful, especially in the realm of dark psychology. If you can appeal to emotion, you are able to sway the rational side of the brain. If people are naturally guided by their emotions, if you can sway them one way or the other, you are far more likely to get the results you want.

Principles of Emotional Influence

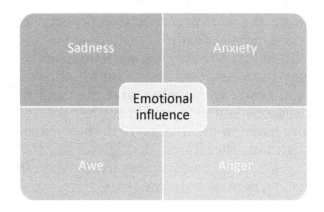

When looking at emotional influence, there are four major motivators that will sway the decision-making process. All emotions sway decision-making to some degree, but ultimately, these four emotions are the most persuasive. Sadness, anxiety, awe, and anger are the most motivating in terms of inspiring action. You may notice that three of the four are negative—and that is intentional. Negative emotions inspire actions that are meant to avoid them in the future. You want to make the negative emotions stop, and oftentimes, you may be able to get a temporary reprieve from the emotion based on decisions you make. For example, sadness can be mitigated, at least temporarily, by doing something that you feel stops the cause of the sadness in the first place.

Sadness

Remember—sadness or sorrow is essentially emotional pain. It involves loss, pain, harm, disappointment, or helplessness and implies a need for support and time to heal. It is a negative influencer—it makes you act in ways that will help you avoid feeling sad for that reason again.

Sadness impacts the brain by making the brain function slower. If you are sad, your brain is essentially fogged—have you ever heard the expression "brain fog?" It is definitely felt when sad. The sadness can be overwhelming, acting as a sort of blanket over the person's mental processes, and makes decision-making more difficult.

Despite this brain fog, however, people tend to make decisions based on short-term benefits. They want to achieve happiness as quickly and easily as possible, and they will make poor long-term decisions simply to avoid further pain of sadness. They are more likely to undervalue both their actual worth as well as the worth of other items, as evidenced by the tendency of people to price items and services lower when feeling sad than when feeling neutral or happy.

All of this culminates in someone who is likely to behave impulsively in ways that they think will assuage their sadness.

Think of commercials that are meant to make you sad in order to get you to donate money. They may claim that you are only donating less than a dollar a day, never mind the fact that even offering up $0.50 a day is still going to add up to $182.5 over the course of a single year. While $0.50 in a donation may seem negligible at best, it adds up over time, culminating into a much larger donation over the course of a year that people might hesitate to give in one lump sum. People are more likely to donate those pennies to that sad ad because they want to make the sadness stop, and they feel that offering up the donation would be enough to make it happen.

Awe
Awe is a state of wonder, typically reserved for things that are seen as more powerful or greater than an individual. Typically, people are left in awe of the vast expanse of space, the depth of the ocean, the mystery and daunting task of assembling Stonehenge, or when viewing other similar objects or meeting people that are influential and seen as superior.

When something or someone leaves you in awe, you are more likely to focus on what is happening at the moment. You are going to feel more aware of what is going on around you, but less aware of the time that is passing. You are in that moment without regard for time and that focus allows you to really appreciate whatever is happening at the moment. This presence at the moment consequentially makes people more willing to give. People will be more likely to help others when in awe and are more likely to make decisions that will be more generous than if they had been feeling anxious or afraid.

This is important—you can usually convince someone to do something by first impressing them with something grandiose. Think of marriage proposals, for example— oftentimes, they are done with big gestures, such as taking someone on a trip to somewhere breathtaking before proposing. There is a reason for this; people are more receptive when they are in awe. If you take your partner somewhere to propose and you can trigger that awe, you are more likely to get the yes you are looking for.

Anxiety

Anxiety goes hand-in-hand with fear. It is typically an emotion that is felt when anticipating a negative result of something and often is joined by nervous behaviors. For example, if you feel anxious about getting into a car accident, you may have a deep-seated fear of dread every time you enter a car or have a sense that you will die if you get into the car.

When attempting to make a decision, people who are actively anxious will struggle to read the situation accurately. They will fail to identify cues or context around them, such as being able to recognize that someone is attempting to manipulate or persuade them to do something that will not be beneficial in the long run. Because anxiety is associated with nervousness, people tend to struggle to identify whether they are in a situation that is stable or that will change in the near future, so they struggle.

When feeling anxious, people are particularly receptive to persuasion and they are far more likely to second-guess their own impulses or reactions. In fact, it has been found that 90% of those who are actively feeling anxious in the moment are likely to seek advice from other people, whereas only 72% of people are willing to do the same in a neutral emotional state.

Lastly, when feeling anxious, you are more inclined to behave selfishly, simply because you are in survival mode. People who are in the throes of anxiety are often far more concerned with their own feelings than of how they may potentially be seen by others, and because of that, they make decisions that will solve their personal conundrum with little regard for the long-term consequences.

Appealing to someone's anxiety can also create fantastic results when attempting to persuade them. Think of a salesperson who wants to sell a newer model car in order to get a larger commission—she might appeal to the other person's anxiety, emphasizing all of the safety features of the newer model and telling a story about someone who got into an accident in the car that the person is looking at and how the accident did not end well at all. Particularly when used against parents, who only want the best for their children, this can sway people to make decisions that they believe will keep them safer because it helps soothe the anxiety they feel. At the moment, feeling anxious and imagining their children being hurt in the other car, the people are more likely to make the impulsive decision to buy the more expensive, newer car model, even if it is a poor long-term decision.

Anger

Anger is incredibly intense. It spurs you to respond to things aggressively and is often used to protect boundaries that are being perceived as being challenged or violated. It allows you to protect those boundaries, cueing for you to protect yourself in the process. Ultimately, anger is incredibly motivating because of self-preservation instincts.

When angry, people are actually more successful at recognizing arguments that are weak or strong. They feel more in control and more able to clearly see where things are wrong or weak compared to strong, compelling arguments. People who are angry feel a call to action—they think that something must be changed, and they will work in order to achieve it. Think of some of the most major social reform that has been accomplished—it is usually around societal issues that instill anger in those who are seeking the change. The people involved were able to clearly and convincingly articulate themselves, which enabled them to make sure the change they wanted occurred.

Ultimately, anger can be used to motivate change for that very reason. If people feel as though they have had their rights infringed upon, or that something is inherently wrong, they are more likely to respond with anger, which, in moderation, becomes the most efficient of the emotions in terms of persuading someone to act. If you are able to instill a sense of righteous indignation in someone else about a topic you are interested in changing, you are able to sway the other person to help you change it as well.

For example, imagine that you are trying to get people to sign a petition about stopping another tax from being passed in your local economy. You may appeal to anger, pointing out how much money it will add to households and how that money will be wrongfully used and how the public should not be expected to foot the bill. When doing that, you are angering other people—they do not want their hard-earned money going to some other inordinate tax that they do not want to pay that will not even benefit them, or the vast majority of people, in any way. When angry, the people are far more inclined to vote against the tax when they likely would have not bothered learning about it or acting upon it at all had you not instilled those feelings of anger.

How to Use Emotional Influence

When attempting to use emotional influence, you have two major steps that can be used—creating or exploiting emotions. You must be able to understand how to do these things in order to successfully emotionally influence someone. Once the emotion is created, or once you have identified it, you will be able to exploit it to your benefit.

Creating emotions
If you are trying to influence someone, you must first create an emotion. Think back to the previous section—the four most driving emotions in terms of motivating someone to do something are anger, fear, awe, and sadness. First, you must install one of these feelings. If you want someone to be enraged, suggest that there will be a result that they do not

like if they do not follow along with what you are asking. To appeal to fear, refer to a worst-case scenario that could occur if they do not do as you are requesting. To appeal to sadness, discuss a sense of loss or pain.

Exploiting emotions
Once the emotions are created, or identified if you did not have to influence the actual emotion, you can begin using it to your advantage. If you see someone that is afraid of what could happen if they crash a cheaper sedan that is within their price range, you may be able to push them toward a more expensive, but also more durable, larger SUV that would withstand most crashes and leave the occupants relatively unscathed. If the other person is already feeling angry about some sort of injustice, you can call that person to action to do whatever you want simply by pointing out how behaving the way you are asking them to do so is going to help fight said injustice.

Reasons to Use Emotional Influence

There are several different reasons that people may appeal to emotional influence in order to get the desired results. Some are selfish while others are done in the best interest of people around them. Regardless of the intent and motivation behind the emotional influence, however, there are several different reasons people may attempt to do this.

Sales
People in sales can benefit greatly from using emotional influence. With this skill mastered, it becomes easier to convince others to buy certain things because you remove the rational thought processes and replace them with emotions. People are typically far more inclined to act emotionally than rationally when they are feeling negative emotions, and by cashing in on that, you may be able to sway purchases ways that they would not have gone before.

For example, imagine you sell mobile phones. Perhaps someone comes in with a toddler in tow. You know you need to up your numbers on insurance and see the perfect opportunity. The person may deny wanting the insurance at first, which you accept. However, you then make mention of how your toddler dropped your phone in the toilet when you turned around for a minute to grab something, and you were so thankful to have insurance since phones are so expensive these days and are absolutely a necessity at this point. People need to be able to check their emails or receive phone calls, and a phone is integral to that. The person may then feel a little worried about having something similar happen, and maybe more receptive to getting the insurance, especially after dropping so much money on such an expensive phone.

Advertising

This is perhaps the most recognizable source for emotional influence. In advertisements, appealing to emotions, as well as making sure to word things in a specific manner that makes the overall impact of a contribution seem less significant. For example, consider an ad that is attempting to raise funds for a certain organization.

It may show all sorts of pictures of people suffering from whatever it is the organization seeks to fight, followed by someone telling you how you can help alleviate the suffering with only $0.50 a day in donations. Sure, that does not seem significant; after all, what are you going to do without $0.50 every day? That adds up quickly—in a year, you are paying over $180. While for some people, that may not be a big deal and it is worth the expense, for others who are struggling, they may be better served saving that $0.50 a day because it could pay for necessities. For some people, that is two months of gasoline costs, or it could buy someone's young child shoes for the entire year, and when you are on a strictly limited income, that $0.50 a day could be a game-changer over the course of a year for someone whose gross income is closer to the poverty level. Someone at the federal poverty line in the United States in 2017, for example, only made about $20,000 a year, with a family of 3 to support. At $20,000 a year, $180 a year becomes just under 1% of their total income. Again, not necessarily significant, but you must consider that for that person, rent and living expenses may already be red-lining them monthly. While the sentiment was good and well-intentioned, it would be likely unviable for someone in poverty to donate even $0.50 a day.

Awareness

When attempting to raise awareness, people frequently appeal to emotions in order to make it memorable. Think about it this way—are you going to remember some statistics listed at you meaninglessly or are you going to remember a story that evokes emotions? Chances are, you will remember the story designed to make you feel something.

For example, someone who is trying to raise awareness to the scourge that is drunk driving, they may tell a story about how entire families are killed in an instant by drunken individuals who chose to drive anyway. They may tell a story about how the family was returning home on Christmas Eve after having gone out to look at Christmas lights, thrilled for the holiday, and in an instant, they were killed by a drunk driver. The point of this is to install that memory within someone else's mind—if they were to ever be in a position where they were debating driving while tipsy, they may recall the emotional story of a family destroyed the night before a major family holiday.

Alternatively, it might be enough to encourage them to stop someone else from driving drunk or to stop a bartender from serving another drink to someone with keys that looks visibly intoxicated.

Politics

Politicians are another user of emotional influence—they are constantly trying to direct negative emotions toward the other party in an attempt to sway people to see their sides.

They may misconstrue and cherry-pick information to make it seem one way when in reality, it is entirely out of context. For example, a politician may point out how some other politician must hate women because he voted a certain way on a certain health issue. The other politician would then construe that, perhaps through cherry-picking, in a way that allows for rage to be directed. If the politician words things, for example, that the other hates women because he voted a certain way and look at how he treats women—it is only a matter of time until he votes that women can no longer vote or deserve equal pay. The rage that is being created then allows for the politician to call a certain demographic to arms, seeking them to come and help keep that other person from attaining votes, which by default, may grant them to the politician who had been pointing out the shortcomings of the other person.

Religion

Religious leaders frequently use emotional influence as well in attempting to get other people to get in line. They oftentimes use threats meant to establish fear, such as using a threat of hell or a lack of access to the afterlife in order to make people live their lives the way that the religious leaders think is necessary. These leaders are able to convince people to follow along blindly through appealing to fear—they may claim that people left to their own devices without religious guidance engage in sins that would make them unworthy of achieving whatever happens afterlife, and that those who sin can corrupt others around them. They push for people to engage in what they deem to be acceptable behaviors because if they do not, they are threatened with damnation or the equivalent. Out of fear, people then decide to follow along with what the religious leaders demand.

Chapter 6: Using Mind Control

When you think of mind control, you may think of someone walking along with a glazed look on her face, not really registering what is happening around her and simply completing orders. It is the epitome of the light is on but no one is home when discussing someone else of their actions and behaviors. This is a work of fiction—people do not actually walk around in such a fashion without significant influence from drugs, but mind control is a fact. It may look incredibly different compared to what you would think of when seeing someone else attempting it, but it is an existing technique. It just happens to look far different than what you may expect. In fact, you may be under the control of someone else as you read this.

Defining Mind Control

Rather than seeing mind control as referring to someone else literally controlling and micromanaging every single move you make; you should look at it as training an animal. Through several techniques, you are able to insert your own thoughts and feelings into another person, or you can create thoughts and feelings that leave the other person quite susceptible to being controlled. You are able to create a person in which even a certain word, a movement, or even the most imperceptible twitch of your lip may be enough to sway them or cue them into behaving in a certain fashion. You essentially remove free will from the other person through your own behaviors, installing your own will instead.

This is a bit of a drawn-out process, however, much like covert manipulation. It must occur slowly and carefully, bit by bit, remaining undetected as it happens. Just as with covert manipulation, the other person never recognizes what is happening, and because you are carefully inching forward with your behaviors and what you expect the other person to tolerate, you are able to put in all of the buttons and conditioning you want before the other person even realizes it is happening. Bit by bit, you are able to take control, and the more control you gain, the worse the other person's self-esteem becomes, and the less likely the other person is to fight back.

It should come as no surprise that this is widely considered unethical. It involves eroding the person's autonomy, taking free will by force, and making the process as undetectable as possible. As it is occurring, particularly if the other person is sneaky enough, there are no real red flags that stand out—it all happens so gradually and the signs are so subtle early on that no one recognizes what is occurring until the damage has been done and the strings are attached. At this point, it becomes incredibly difficult for the other person to begin differentiating between her own thought process and the one that was artificially installed that the other person is essentially stuck—they will likely need professional help to disentangle the undercover thoughts.

Using Mind Control

When you are attempting to exert control over someone else's mind, you will likely have your work cut out for you. However, if you manage to spend the time doing so, you are likely to create results that you are seeking to create. Remember, just because this is using mental manipulation does not mean you have to use it to harm others—you can use this knowledge to sway people into behaviors that are beneficial to everyone or use it in an ethical manner.

Understanding the target
The first step in attempting mind control is learning to understand the other person. You need to understand what they are doing and what their behavioral patterns are if you hope to get in and change them into whatever it is you wish

they were. For example, if you know the other person is likely to behave aggressively when angry, you will be able to predict the angry reactions. You are also likely to understand what is causing those angry reactions and why those angry reactions will be felt in a wide range of circumstances.

Identifying weaknesses
When you know how the other person behaves and what their emotional triggers seem to be, you can begin identifying weaknesses in it. When you know that they have certain triggers, you can utilize those, but artificially create a reaction you are looking for. Remember the parts of emotional influence that discussed how certain emotions impact persuasive ability? You can take advantage of that. You may know that the other person gets angry and those angry people are not likely to be very open to persuasion convincing them to do the opposite of whatever it was that they were doing, but you may know how to sway that anger into guilt, which is closely related to sadness and leaves people far more receptive. You need to understand these chain reactions in people and how you can use them to your benefit.

Breaking self-esteem
Just as with covert manipulation, the lower the other person's self-esteem, the easier they will be to control. You can use similar steps as discussed there to lower self-esteem in conjunction with the above steps. When you have the other person feeling low self-esteem, insecurity, and one of the more receptive to persuasion emotions, you can begin using them against the other person to really install the strings you will need to control them.

Using their emotions
As you begin to install strings and begin influencing someone else is to do so through emotions. Each of the following emotions can create different behavioral patterns in other people and if you use them effectively, you will be able to control the other people in your life. Both people in whom you

have installed strings and people you need to change behaviors of instantly can be swayed to do as you desire if you understand how to leverage these emotions.

- **Fear:** Both strangers and those you are attempting to keep under your control can be motivated by fear. You can use fear in an attempt to coerce or intimidate a person into giving you what you want, whether it is compliance or be given something, or you can use it when attempting to end a confrontation. For example, if someone comes up to you aggressively, attempting to get you to give up your wallet, you stand the chance of intimidating them back. Take a position of confidence and authority and stare him down, shouting back and the other person may be shocked, and then frightened, by your reaction, and you did not have to do anything in preparation of doing so.

- **Guilt:** Guilt can be leveraged with several people. You can convince people around you to do as you are requesting out of obligation and guilt, such as requesting that someone lends you money and appealing to guilt and obligation when they resist, with phrases about how family must stick together, and that you'll really miss your home when you miss it due to inability to pay rent. You can also use guilt to disarm anger as well—imagine that your boss is yelling at you because you have failed to do something he needed. If you can make him feel guilty for his anger, such as with your own body language or telling him a personal detail he did not know about you, you can instill a sense of guilt in him, which is far more likely to get him to try to help you, completely defusing the anger.

- **Ego:** Most people have some sense of ego, but others have larger ones. If you are dealing with someone with an inflated ego, you can use it to keep them under your thumb. For example, if you have a friend that is refusing to follow through with something, he had said he would do, you can shrug and say that no one expected him to do so anyway, and you are not surprised. Out of a desire to protect his ego, you may find him working harder to prove you wrong, which consequentially, also got you the desired result.

- **Addiction:** Just as how people can be entirely enslaved to their chemical addictions, you can addict someone to you. Through methods such as love bombing, mirroring, and understanding how to seduce someone, you can essentially convince someone that they are in love with you. Once they are there, you can use that love to keep them in line, threatening to withhold it or leave the other person if they are not going to obey whatever it is you are asking them to do.
- **Anger:** Sometimes, inciting anger is the best way to get someone under control, but usually, it will involve inciting anger that is specifically directed at someone else. If you want your girlfriend to stop talking to a friend that you feel may be a threat to your relationship, for example, you could tell your girlfriend things that you think are bound to anger and frustrate her. The more you can induce anger in your girlfriend directed toward her friend, the more likely it is that she will cut off that friend.

Techniques for Mind Control

Of course, your knowledge of how to control other people is not complete without a list of techniques that can be used to do so. This section will provide you with some of the most commonly used mind control methods that have not yet been discussed. Remember, most of what you saw in the covert manipulation chapter can also be used here.

Limited choices
How do you deal with an unruly child that is constantly expecting way too much, or demanding that something does not happen? You give them the illusion of choice—provide

them with two or three options that are acceptable to you and present them as the only options available. Are those the only options available? No, of course not, but when you restrict them like that, you are far more likely to see the result you want. The same goes with adults that you are trying to manipulate. If you want your girlfriend to do something to help you, for example, you can offer her the choice of doing what you want her to do or leaving the relationship. Are these the only two choices? No—the relationship could also continue without doing the behavior, but you do not make that an option on the table. By narrowing the choices down to two things, you are able to force a decision.

Repetition

People remember things that have been repeated to them over and over again in natural contexts. Do you remember that this book has advocated for the ethical use of the skills within it? That is because it has been repeated in the hopes of you absorbing the information. If you want someone to do a certain thing or think a certain way, by casually bringing it up over a period of time, you are more likely to get the other person to take up that belief as well. For example, your friend may not really like a certain brand that you are enthusiastic about. You could repeatedly tell him how awesome the band is over the course of a week or two. Then, the next time you casually play music from that band, he may have internalized the idea that it is likable and actually enjoy whatever it was that you were playing.

Constantly changing the subject

When you are changing the subject constantly on someone, you are making it impossible for them to keep up with what is being said. When you make it impossible to keep up with the conversation, you make it difficult for the other person to sufficiently defend him or herself from whatever claims you are making. For example, if you are in the middle of an argument with your spouse over her believing that you do not contribute enough around your home, you can suddenly spitfire several different problems you may have with your spouse. This does two things—it changes the subject and focus away from you and puts your spouse on the defensive. When you spouse is busy defending herself, you can keep her off balance, so to speak, throwing several different complaints before she can defend herself, and eventually, the end result is her overwhelmed and quite possibly more willing to listen to what you are saying simply out of desperation. If she could not defend herself and grow flustered, she may feel like whatever you have said is actually true.

Emotional and covert manipulation

The techniques used in both emotional influence and covert manipulation can be used in order to control other people's minds. You can use the skills carefully and manage to control and influence what the other person is thinking before the other person is even aware of you doing it. If you feel the need, take a refresher and overlook those categories now for several other techniques.

Mirroring

Mirroring was something mentioned in body language, but it is also an incredibly useful manipulation tool. When you mirror someone else, you are able to convince them that they are interested in you simply because you are interested in them. They begin to consider you someone that should be trusted simply because your body language says you can be trusted. After you have been mirroring the other person, you will begin to notice the other person mirroring you as well— this is a sign that they are interested in you and is an opening to begin working your magic.

Changing goalposts

One of the simplest methods used in controlling the actions of someone else is through constantly changing the goalposts on the other person. With this method, nothing the other person does is ever good enough for you. If you complain that your spouse does not cook enough, for example, they may begin to cook regularly, but you would then complain that the cooking is poor. You would continuously up your standards out of reach of whatever the other person is doing. The other person is then constantly in a state of pursuing standards that he or she will never actually be able to attain, leaving them within your grasp.

Chapter 7: Deception

Do you recognize when those around you are deceiving you? Perhaps you would like to be able to understand how to deceive others for your own gain, or you want to be able to identify when someone else attempts to deceive you. Regardless of your reasons for your interest, deception is an incredibly useful skill to understand. Remember, when you understand how something like deception works, you are able to also defend yourself from deception's grasp. You will be able to prevent it from happening to you simply because you know how it is done and what to look out for.

Remember, deception is almost never ethical—it involves deliberately lying or misrepresenting something for selfish gain, and should be avoided when possible if you are attempting to remain ethical. Nevertheless, there are sometimes situations in which deception is the best way to maintain control and protect yourself. If you ever face one of those instances, being skilled in the art of deception could be useful. In fact, some professions learn this skill simply because it can be useful, such as when trying to convince someone who is holding people hostage to give up, or when attempting to talk someone down in order to escape. There are several different ways to deceive, and understanding all of them can be beneficial.

Defining Deception

Before you learn how to deceive other people, however, you must first learn how to define it. Deception is a psychological phenomenon in which someone is attempting to mislead another. It involves attempts meant to trick other people through actions, behaviors, or words into believing something other than the truth. It does occur sometimes in ethical fashion, such as when attempting to perform clinical trials to be able to account for biases, but it should be avoided when not absolutely necessary.

Ultimately, the purpose of deception is to mislead others or promote a belief that is untrue. There are several different ways this can occur, and some people claim that certain types of deception are more dishonest than others, justifying some kinds while abhorring others. However, deception can be considered a form of fraud and can even be punishable in criminal law depending on the severity, and it could also be seen as grounds for civil suits as well.

Types of Deception and How to Use Them

When deceiving others, there are several ways that you can choose to do so. With a wide arsenal of potential deceptive techniques and possible ways that you could choose to deceive others, there is never a shortage of possible deceptions to create. You can, for example, lie, or omit certain facts—both are still active deception, even though one involves lying and the other involves simply not saying anything. Anything that is intended to distort or misrepresent the truth counts as deception. This section will give you a list of six of the most common types of deception as well as examples of each.

Lies

Perhaps the most well-known of the ways to deceive others, lying involves blatantly stating something that is not true. It involves answering in ways that are intentionally dishonest in order to give the other person false information about whatever the individual is hoping to use deceptively. For example, imagine that you have to go to a party, but you really would rather stay home and sleep or do something on your own.

You know that your friend, who is the guest of honor, will be crushed if you do not show up, so you instead make up some sort of lie that allows you to get out of going. You may say that your stomach is upset and you are worried about making the other people at the party sick in order to offer up an excuse that you think the other person will believe, even though in reality, you simply do not want to go for your own reasons.

When lying, there are two main kinds: Lying by the commission and lying by omission. The first, lying by commission, involves adding something false to what you are saying. This is lying in its truest form and is entirely dishonest. Lying by omission, on the other hand, involves leaving information out altogether. When lying by omission, you will not offer up any information that you know is relevant if it has not been directly asked for.

Equivocations

Equivocations involve indirect answers or ambiguity. When attempting to use equivocation, you are essentially using language that is vague or ambiguous in an attempt to hide the truth. This is frequently used in politics in order to hide the truth or to avoid answering in a manner that would be unpopular. It can also be used during court, with attorneys recommending the person on the stand using ambiguous, equivocal language in order to avoid actually admitting guilt while also not lying. It enables the truth to be hidden behind ambiguity, granting plausible deniability.

For example, imagine that a politician is talking about how a new tax would impact everyone. When asked how much each category would be paying, the answer is that the upper class is paying more while the lower class is paying less—which may technically be true in sheer amounts of income but may not be accurate in terms of how much discretionary income they may have available. It is unclear whether the politician means that the lower class will be paying a lower percentage of disposable income or a lower quantity overall.

Concealments

When concealing the truth, people omit certain parts of information. They will tell the parts of something that are good or relevant while simultaneously leaving out parts that they think would hurt what they are trying to get. They may answer indirectly when asked a question in an attempt to skirt around answering the actual question, which enables them to hide information they feel may be detrimental.

For example, imagine that you have just asked your coworker if he has stolen something off of your desk. He may look at you in shock and disgust before declaring loudly, "Do I look like someone who would steal?" He did not directly answer the question, instead of implying an answer without ever having to actually lie. Oftentimes, people will feel like this is not lying simply because they never said anything untrue, even though they did intentionally avoid saying the truth in the situation. While not necessarily lying, it is still an attempt to hide the truth.

Exaggerations
When exaggerating, the truth is stretched in some way. At some point, it goes from an innocent exaggeration into the territory of deception. When the exaggeration involves boasting or bolstering your own value or importance to the point that it could be seen as a false advertisement of yourself, it is often considered deceptive. It can also be deceptive when you are over-exaggerating to elicit pity, such as the case of a child who, during a fight, goes running to the adult in charge, crying and making herself look pitiful while blaming the other person for starting the fight, even though she may have been the provoker from the start.

When you are beginning to exaggerate injuries, discomforts, or pain to avoid responsibility, you are also being deceptive. Overall, the biggest difference between the deceptive exaggerations and simple exaggerations as a joke or meant innocently is intent—when exaggerating deceptively, you are doing so to hide something or to misconstrue the truth. When exaggerating innocently, people understand that you are using it as hyperbole.

Understatements
In contrast to exaggerations, some people understate, meaning they minimize the situation in order to make the truth seem less difficult to accept. When understating something, you are able to convince other people that whatever has happened is not nearly as bad as others may assume at first glance. It can be used in innocent manners, such as to convey comedy, modesty, or politeness, or it can be used deceptively in order to misconstrue the truth.

For example, imagine you are babysitting. The child you are caring for runs into a corner when zipping around the house, leaving a huge goose egg on his forehead and what looks like the beginnings of a black eye. You may send a quick text message to the child's parents, saying that the child got hurt a little bit, but it is not a big deal, downplaying and understating the injury in order to not alarm the parents because you really need the babysitting money and you do not want them to come home and pick up the child, who is doing fine besides the obvious bruising. Of course, when they get home, they will see the injury and be furious at it being described as a tiny bump, but you were able to babysit the full length of time to get the full amount of money.

Simulation
In the simulation, you intentionally present things in a false manner. When doing this, usually you use either fabrication or distraction. Each of these is set to deceive the other party in some way. For example, fabrication is when someone appears to be someone or something that he or she is not. You may present yourself as an expert in on a topic in hopes of convincing others that you are in order to appeal to authority. You may also pretend to have a license or qualification that you do not have. With distraction, on the other hand, you distract someone from the truth with something else that may

or may not be true as well. For example, if someone is attempting to keep someone from discovering that their degree is falsified, they may instead offer up some other credential when the degree is being questioned in hopes of distracting the other person altogether.

Lies
- The sky is orange, not blue.

Equivocations
- The poor will pay less than the rich with this new tax scheme.

Concealments
- Does it look like I would have done that?

Exaggerations
- I was the most important member of the team-- they would have failed without me.

Understatements
- "The car just has a scratch"-- even though the scratch ruined the paint across the entire right side.

Simulations
- "I am licensed to perform this task"-- even though the person is not.

Recognizing Deception

Now that you understand the most commonly used deceptive strategies, you are free to begin recognizing deception as it occurs. Along with looking for the previously mentioned strategies, you should also be looking at several other signs as well. Even those well-versed in deception are frequently caught by those who know what to look for and how to prevent it from becoming a problem. When you are ready to begin identifying those in your life that are deceiving you, or if you suspect that someone close to you has already been attempting to do so, follow the following steps. Ultimately, you want to get an idea of what that person's normal behavior looks like, use that knowledge to look for other signs of stress, pay attention to body language, pay attention to vocabulary, and listen to the voice.

Create a picture of the individual's baseline
Firstly, you must get an idea of what that person's neutral body looks like. Some people are naturally anxious, and you do not want to mistake their natural body language as signs of lying or dishonesty. Because different people will naturally orient their bodies in different ways with different expected results, you want to ensure that you are familiar enough with what that person looks like neutrally. In order to get an idea of what that person's neutral body language looks like, attempt to carry a normal conversation with the person, asking questions that people would have no real reason to lie about. For example, in interviews, you could ask someone about their hobbies in an attempt to get to know the person a little bit more, or you could ask questions about the person's age, date of birth, name or other similar questions to get an idea if she is touching her face out of nervousness or out of deceit.

Look for unique stress signals
After creating a baseline to compare to, you are free to begin identifying whether the person is lying to you. Look for signs that indicate stress, as lying is generally quite stressful on the body. The heart rate and breathing rate will generally speed up, and while you may not be able to see or hear the increase in heart rate, you may be able to pick up on the change in breathing. Likewise, you may be able to recognize that their heart rate has increased simply due to the presence of self-soothing behaviors, such as biting or licking the lips, touching the face, or messing with jewelry. Especially if those behaviors were not present beforehand, it is quite likely that these distressed signals imply that the other person is lying to you. You may even notice that the person freezes up for a fraction

of a second after you have asked something—this is a flash of the fight-flight-freeze response and is a sign that they have been caught in a lie, even if it only lasts for the briefest moment before fading away.

Watch body language

Remember the list of body language that was provided back in Chapter 2? Now is a good time to review it to really solidify that you understand the most common cues. Beyond those most common signs of deception, there is also a list of nonverbal language that, when clustered together, almost always implies lying and dishonesty. There are four parts to this:

- **Touching hands:** The individual may fidget with his or her hands repeatedly, perhaps disguising this behavior by messing with a watch or wedding ring.
- **Touching the face:** When touching the face, particularly the eyes or mouth, the person is cuing that they are trying to hide something.
- **Keeping arms crossed:** By crossing arms, the individual makes a barrier between himself and the other person.
- **Leaning back:** Leaning back puts some distance between the individual and the other person, which is desired during periods of dishonesty.

When you see all four of these behaviors happening together, there is a good chance the other person is lying. Of course, this is not an exact science, and you cannot look at someone and know beyond a preponderance of a doubt that they are lying, but this cluster of body language is significant enough to recommend you begin looking for other signs of lying.

Listen to word choice

Listen to how the person is wording things and seek out any signs of the above types of deception. Now that you understand how they are done, you may be more likely to notice when someone is over-exaggerating or understating something to get a specific reaction, or that they are being ambiguous in order to hide something.

Listen to tone and pitch
When people are stressed, their voice usually becomes higher in pitch. The reasoning behind this is due to the stress and tension felt—when you stress, your body is tense, and when you are tense, your vocal cords are also kept tense, which makes them produce a higher pitch. When this happens, people may also be caught drinking more water in an attempt to lessen dry mouth, which is also a result of the same tension and stress that tightened the vocal cords in the first place.

Chapter 8: Seduction with Dark Psychology

Seduction involves enticing someone else into a relationship or into sexual behavior—it could literally be seen as the art of winning over someone who may not have originally wanted to be won over in the first place and is typically used solely based upon physical or sexual attraction. It can be a skill that can be quite beneficial if you are not looking to settle down into a long-term relationship, or even if you are seeking to rekindle the spark with your spouse. After all, the language of love is universal—everyone wants to feel loved and wanted.

Defining Seduction

Ultimately, seduction is the act of one person leading another person astray—in fact, the etymology of the word seduce comes from the Latin word meaning "leading astray" or "to corrupt." With that in mind, you can more-or-less deduce that the initial context of seduction is quite negative. It involves essentially swaying the other person to do something that they may not have been okay within other situations. Nevertheless, it is something that has persevered through thousands of years of humanity, and it clearly is not going anywhere.

It is important to note one particular nuance—there is a fine line between rape and seduction. Rape involves forcible sexual contact with another person against the other person's will while seduction is pursuing another person, potentially against their will, until they do consent. It is important to note that when attempting to seduce another person, you must remember to respect consent or a lack thereof.

Choosing a Target

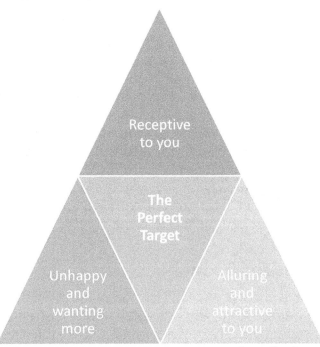

Perhaps the most important step toward seducing another person is discovering the proper target. As briefly touched upon, the most important thing to remember is that the other person should absolutely be receptive to the idea of being seduced. If the person does not seem as though he or she would ever fall for your tactics, or they resist when you attempt, pushing forward and attempting to force the point is crossing the lines from seduction into coercion. Remember, in seduction, you want to chase the target until the target is chasing you instead—this means that you can pursue the other person, but you are only pursuing them insofar as to cause them to instead pursue you. If they will never pursue you, you will never be able to seduce them and it is time to move on to someone else.

Beyond being receptive to your charms and attempts to seduce, the best targets are the ones in which you sense avoid that you are able to fill—they may be lonely or self-conscious and want to be wanted. You can take advantage of that desire and use it to your own benefit, choosing to pursue them knowing that you are fulfilling a part of them that they never expected would be filled. These people are typically isolated, unhappy, or they will be able to be made into an isolated, unhappy individual with very little effort from you. Remember, someone who is perfectly content with life is not going to be interested in being seduced. You want to make sure that the person you wish to seduce is unhappy, but also that they are appealing to you as well. After all, unless they evoke intense emotions from you, you are not likely to keep an interest in the target. You are not going to enjoy the chase or the thrill if you feel like the target is not right.

Techniques for Seducing

Once you have chosen your target and ensured that the other person will be receptive, you are ready to begin attempting the process of seduction. There is a myriad of available techniques you can use in order to seduce another person—it is simply a matter of deciding which will work best for you and which you think that you would like to use. Take a look over this list and begin to make a plan for what would work best for you and your target. Remember, no two targets are the same, and because of that, there is no one-size-fits-all approach to how to seduce the target. Ultimately, you are following the same basic steps—identify a target, make them feel vulnerable, make them interested in you, and reap the rewards. How you get through those steps can vary greatly from person to person.

Mixed signals
Ultimately, you want to make sure that you stand out to the person you are attempting to seduce. What better way to do this than to send mixed signals to the person? When you send mixed signals, you make yourself interesting—you are a walking contradiction and that catches people's attention. You

84

will be fresh and exciting, and people naturally gravitate toward fresh and exciting. By showing a mix of qualities, some of which that may seem very contradictory, you will be surprising, which will direct attention to you.

When you do this, you want to make yourself interesting. Think about what your target would like and strive for that— perhaps you want to have that tough-guy approach while also showing that you have a tender side when you stop to feed that hungry dog lurking in the alleyway, or you help carry an old woman's groceries inside. You can be serious, but comical at the same time—knowing the difference between when to be down-to-earth and focused on success, work, or other serious behaviors, but also knowing how to let loose and not being afraid to do so. When you show a wide mix of different qualities, you show the other person that you have depth, and that depth can be quite attractive, especially if the other person feels mystified or confused by you.

Make yourself look more desirable

Sometimes, one of the easier ways to convince someone else to act is to make it look like someone else is interested. Remember the principle of scarcity? This is appealing to that—you are literally making it look like someone else is interested in you in hopes of instilling jealousy in the other person and encouraging them to pursue you quickly.

Ultimately, people are far more interested in people that seem to attract other people. If you want to get your target more interested in you, you need to make it clear that others are also interested in you. You can do this by making yourself seem desirable—as you become more desirable in the eyes of the other person, the more likely they are to act accordingly and pursue you, even if prior, they had never shown much interest in you in the first place. After all, if everyone is interested in you, there must be something special about you, and the other person is naturally going to want to see what it is.

Make the other person anxious

As already briefly touched upon, people who are perfectly happy with how life has been for them are not likely to want to be seduced. In fact, they will have no interest because they do not feel as though they are missing out on anything in particular. Sometimes, you can skip this step by simply looking for someone who is actively showing signs of discontent and anxiety, but other times, you have to go out of your way to make the other person feel anxious.

Of course, you are going to want to do this as covertly as possible—you do not want the other person knowing what you are doing, or they are not likely to want to pursue you. After all, very few people want to be with someone they know is actively attempting to sabotage them. Instead, revisit the chapters on covert manipulation, emotional influence, and mind control if you are unsure of the ways you would use to slowly but systematically destroy self-esteem to create a better-controlled target.

Adapt to the other person's preferences

When you are attempting to seduce someone, but you are not particularly interested in a long-term relationship, perhaps the easiest way to do so is through creating an artificial sense of self. You essentially want to take on whatever traits your target will find attractive solely because you are attempting to attract the target. You will not need to permanently develop a passionate love for underwater basket weaving, but you should absolutely pretend to be interested in it if it is something that the target is also interested in.

Sweet talking

People tend to be poor listeners, particularly if they are not hearing what they want to hear. When you recognize this fact, you can then begin to draw attention from others simply by telling them what they want to hear. When they are hearing what they want to hear coming from you, they are going to pay attention—after all, why wouldn't they if you are actively

86

providing them with whatever they desire at the moment? In order to seduce, you must master the art of figuring out what they want you to say and delivering those words. You will inflate their egos, make them feel better, and addict them to the words you whisper gently into their ears, and they will find themselves far more eager to follow.

Temptation

There is a reason temptation rears its head in so many different stories and myths—it is incredibly persuasive. When you tempt someone, showing them the tiniest glimpse of what they could have if they went with you, you are essentially teasing the other person. The other person may become fixated on that tiny glimpse, desiring more and seeking it out. You essentially create a desire in the other person that they cannot deny or fight off—if you can discover the one thing that will spark that desire, they will be likely to follow you if you offer the potential to achieve the thing that they desire in the first place.

Parent your target

Ultimately, people are more likely to relate to their best memories—for most, the most joyous occasions happened in childhood and involve parents in some fashion. You can bring back those feelings if you are able to put yourself in a parental role without making it obvious. Make a point to offer some sort of care for the other person, wording it as you being concerned for their wellbeing and wanting to help out in any way possible, and you can likely send them back to those feelings of secure attachment, which of course, makes them far more likely to pursue you.

Insinuations

Learning how to insinuate things—meaning being able to install an idea into someone's mind through subtle, indirect language, can be particularly effective when attempting to seduce another person. In doing so, you create uncertainty, and in uncertainty, you essentially sway the person to do as you are requesting. You can suggest that you are interested in the other person without ever actually saying anything, which may actually make the other person interested in following you in the first place.

Suspense
When in suspense, the target is going to be enthralled with you—they are not sure what to expect, and that makes you interesting. They want to pursue you simply to find out what will happen next because you are so unpredictable. If you want to maintain this suspense, you must constantly be fabricating ways to keep the suspense going. Always look to do things that are unexpected simply because it will help keep other people, and your target, interested in you. They will be attracted by your spontaneity and interested in following you while you remain comfortably in control of where the relationship is heading.

Mystery and poeticism
You want yourself to be a sort of an enigma to the target you seek to seduce. After all, once you become familiar in the target's life, the target could potentially be glad for periods of time in which you are not present. They may realize that something they are doing would not be interesting to you, or you would complicate things, and when that realization occurs, you are no longer in control. In order to avoid this, you must make yourself mysterious and elusive. Make your presence exciting, mysterious, and even poetic—you could create associations between yourself and other items or objects. For example, you could create an association between yourself and a certain species of bird—every time the person sees that particular kind of bird, they will think of you. The more they are thinking of you, the more likely they will be to follow you.

Playing the victim
This is a difficult one to manage—you must tow a fine line between too much-attempted manipulation and not enough. If

you go overboard, the other person is likely to be suspicious of you, which can be enough of a reason for them to avoid you altogether. The easiest way to give yourself access to the other person's weaknesses without raising suspicion, then, is to make the other person feel that they are superior. If you can make the other person think that they are the superior one and that you are the more vulnerable person, they are not going to be as alarmed by your attempts to manipulate and seduce. For example, if you make yourself vulnerable, and then make it a point to cry to the other person, knowing it will guilt them into giving you your way, it will look more natural than if you had never cried or shown vulnerability before.

Balancing highs and lows

Oftentimes, the worst mistake people make when attempting to seduce others is being too nice. While kindness and niceties are nice, they are not particularly helpful or beneficial with seduction. You become boring, predictable, and the other person sees no reason to keep trying. You are boring simply because you always want to please the other person. Instead, you can attempt to create lows to make the highs seem better. If you start a fight or break up with the other person, for example, the highs will seem far higher when compared to the low point of that fight than if the highs are compared to your neutral state of trying to please them. You can do this in several ways—make the other person feel bad. You could make them feel guilty for not inviting you out to dinner, or make them feel insecure in the relationship with that breakup. With the negatives occurring, the target will be far more likely to welcome the highs and kindnesses with open arms when they are compared to being broken up with.

Keep trying—within reason

Most of the people you will encounter are interested in being seduced, even if they do not say so. After all, it is such a common fantasy for people that it is a frequently recurring trope, in both films and novels for both men and women. If the other person does not seem receptive to seduction, you should keep trying or move on to someone else if you do not want to waste the time.

Conclusion

Ultimately, everything you have learned within this book toes the line between ethical and unethical. Depending on the context and the way you decide to use the knowledge in this book, you can remain a moral, ethical individual, or you could use the knowledge to your own advantage, using it however you see fit in order to get what you want. The choice is yours— what you do with the knowledge is on you and you alone.

Within this book, you were given plenty of information about ways to manipulate, persuade, influence, and seduce. Each of the techniques provided in this book could have some sort of use that could be beneficial somehow, even if unconventionally, and because of that, each technique discussed is quite valuable. You should remember how the book emphasized body language in particular—understanding how people communicate, both verbally and nonverbally is perhaps one of the greatest skills an individual could develop.

Further, this book emphasized the importance of recognizing the signs of how to seduce other people. While seduction is not necessarily evil or bad in any way, it absolutely can be if you continue to harass and pursue someone who is clearly not interested in being pursued. You were given the signs of what a good target looks like, as well as how to achieve seduction.

From here, you have a wide range of choices. You can choose to move forward with attempting to manipulate and persuade those around you for your own gain. You can choose to use your newfound knowledge to protect yourself from other people's attempts to persuade or manipulate. You can use your knowledge to better yourself and further your own enjoyment in life. Regardless of what you choose to go do, remember the most crucial parts of this book.

Remember that body language is essential to reading people, and reading people is half the battle of manipulation and persuasion.

Remember that ultimately, slow and steady does win the manipulative race and that there is no rush to push your mind control attempts further than necessary when attempting to install all of the buttons and strings that will serve you well.

Remember that deception, while relatively easy to attempt to hide, has several different cues and tells that you can use to read another person during attempts to lie.

Good luck as you move forward in your journey; hopefully you will find some use within the pages of this book, and the knowledge included here will be beneficial to you in some significant way, shape, or form.

CPSIA information can be obtained
at www.ICGtesting.com
Printed in the USA
LVHW050555211220
674727LV00007B/120

9 781914 062773